Book Editors
Talk to Writers

Now available:

Book Editors
Talk to Writers

JUDY MANDELL

JOHN WILEY & SONS, INC.
New York · Chichester · Brisbane · Toronto · Singapore

For Jerry, Pam, Scott,
Kim, Jim, Elizabeth,
and, littlest but not least, Joshua

This text is printed on acid-free paper.

Copyright © 1995 by Judy Mandell
Published by John Wiley & Sons, Inc.

This publication is designed to provide accurate and authoritative information in regard to
the subject matter covered. It is sold with the understanding that the publisher is not
engaged in rendering professional services. If legal, accounting, medical, psychological, or
any other expert assistance is required, the services of a competent professional person
should be sought.

Library of Congress Cataloging-in-Publication Data:

Mandell, Judy, 1939–
    Book editors talk to writers / Judy Mandell.
        p.   cm.
    ISBN 0-471-00391-3 (pbk. : alk. paper)
    1. Authorship—Marketing.   2. Editors—United States—Interviews.
    3. Book editors—United States—Interviews.   I. Title.
    PN161.M28   1995
    808'.02—dc20   94-41641

Printed in the United States of America.

10 9 8 7 6 5 4 3 2 1

Acknowledgments

To the wonderful editors
who graciously gave me so much of their precious time.

Thank you.

Thank you for the explanations, the exhortations, the revelations, the dedication, and the inspiration.

Despite your overwhelming workloads and production deadlines, you eagerly talked to me.

For that I am grateful.

And mega-thank-yous to PJ Dempsey, my editor at John Wiley, who showed me, in eloquent English, that writers need editors.

Contents

**Part Two
Specialized Books**

Preface

Several years ago, as I was working on my book, *Fiction Writer's Guidelines*, I received a phone call from an editor. "I'm not sending you our guidelines because writers won't read them anyway. I'm up to my eyeballs with editing, constantly worried about production deadlines, and perpetually behind. I don't have time for freelancers who send inappropriate proposals. That's all I have to say." She slammed down the phone. That unpleasant phone call spurred me to investigate the relationship between writers and editors.

It's extremely difficult for freelance writers to get published. If writers knew what it was like to be on the receiving end of queries and proposals, if they knew what editors wanted and didn't want, I surmised that they could be more successful.

I wrote a feature article for *Writer's Digest* magazine in order to seek the truth about writers, editors, and book publishing. I asked dozens of editors throughout the country for the inside scoop. "What do you look for in a proposal? Give me the negatives as well as the positives. What turns you on? What turns you off? What makes you love one author and hate another? What makes one proposal irresistible and another a loser? How do you feel about phone calls from authors? Do you deal directly with authors? Would you rather deal with an author or an agent?" The success of that article spurred me to write *Book Editors Talk to Writers*.

My goal for *Book Editors Talk to Writers* is to help writers get published by better understanding how editors think and how publishing works. Although I have written the book with the assumption that my readers know little of publishing, much of the information should interest and inform the most sophisticated author.

Each chapter of *Book Editors Talk to Writers* begins with a short bio of the editor and covers a different topic. The book is divided into two major sections—Part 1: What Every Writer Wants to Know (But May Be Afraid to Ask) and Part 2: Specialized Books. The information in Part 1 should interest all readers. Although much of the material in Part 2 applies to all writers, readers can seek out certain chapters.

I posed to every editor what I thought were the most-asked questions and problems that writers encounter. "How do editors usually acquire books? Why do so few books make the best-seller list? Do all writers need agents? What if the manuscript isn't accepted by the publisher? What about book promotions? What about advances? What are the royalties and what are they based on?"*

I asked editors to reveal "the truth" about book publishing—"What is the best way for writers to get published? What are your pet peeves about authors? What do you advise writers in search of a publisher?" I always asked editors to fill in what I may have left out.

Most chapters end with pet peeves and advice to authors so that readers can quickly find the inside scoop and compare editors' points of view.

I used a question-and-answer format because it reveals the editor's persona and because readers can easily skip to topics of interest.

Because jargon is ubiquitous in book publishing, I have placed Charles Spicer's chapter on publishing lingo and Brian DeFiore's chapter on contracts at the beginning of the book so that readers can decipher the distinctive terms found throughout this book.

The *Literary Market Place* (*LMP*), often referred to in the text, is an annual directory of American book publishers and related services published by R. R. Bowker.

* (You'll notice that royalties can be paid on either the list price or net price of a book, depending on a publisher's mode of accounting. "List" simply means that the author's royalty is calculated on the cover price of the book. So, an author receiving a 10 percent list royalty on a $10 book will get $1.00 per book sold. "Net" means that the author's royalty is calculated on the amount the publisher nets after discounts to the bookseller. Net royalties are usually paid by the publisher of textbooks or professional books. Discounts for these are usually very low [10–30 percent] and the list price is generally much higher because of the specialized nature of the subject matter. If a publisher of general trade books offers a net royalty [and their standard discount is in the 40–50 percent range] they usually compensate by paying the author a higher royalty rate so that in the end the author receives about the same amount either way.)

Part One

What Every Writer
Wants to Know
(But May Be Afraid to Ask)

Publishing Lingo

The Slush Pile, Over the Transom, Book Auctions, Remainder Sales, Positioning Books, Mass Market, Trade Books, Backlist, Frontlist, Midlist, Genre, and More

CHARLES SPICER, SENIOR EDITOR

St. Martin's Press, Inc.
New York

CHARLES SPICER has been senior editor in the trade division at St. Martin's Press since 1987. His eclectic list includes commercial fiction and nonfiction, paperback and hardcover. Spicer runs St. Martin's True Crime Library, which publishes original paperbacks; reprints of St. Martin's hardcover true crime books; instant books about recent, highly publicized cases; and true crime books purchased from other houses.

St. Martin's Press, owned by Macmillan, U.K., was started in the late 1950s as a small line to distribute books. It has since become one of the largest trade publishing houses in the United States. According to Spicer, St. Martin's receives thousands of proposals each year.

☐ **What is the slush pile?**
All the manuscripts and proposals that come in with no editor's name attached to them. Some houses refuse to read slush.

□ **Is a proposal slush if it has an editor's name on it, but that editor does not know the author?**

It's a step above slush. If it has an editor's name on it, it's more effective. If it gets to my office with my name on it, I'll look at it. If it's something I'm interested in, I'll treat it the way I treat anything else.

□ **What is "over the transom"?**

In publishing, over the transom is the same as slush. The transom is the edge of a boat. Something thrown into a boat from the sea comes in over the transom.

□ **What is backlist?**

Backlist are the books that have an ongoing sale year after year after year—the books that sell and sell and sell. The backlist is the backbone of any publishing house.

□ **What is frontlist?**

Frontlist are the new books coming out—every book's debut. Some may go on to live as backlist books.

□ **What is midlist?**

Midlist is fiction or nonfiction that does not have best-seller potential. Houses are increasingly dropping midlist, because of the low return on investment.

□ **What is genre?**

Genre are specific types of books, usually paperback. They include romance, true crime, western, and military books.

□ **What is trade publishing?**

Trade publishing is commercial publishing. Trade publications are general interest books as opposed to scholarly and reference, or academic, although there is some crossover.

□ **What are trade paperback books?**

Trade paperback books can be hardcover size, with paper covers.

□ **What is mass market?**

Mass market are rack-size paperbacks that you see in drugstores, supermarkets—everywhere.

□ **What is a book auction, and how does it work?**

A book auction is conducted by telephone, and can last one day, two days, or a week, but usually takes place in a day.

An agent sends a proposal to several publishing houses, with a specified closing date. Before that date, editors must read the proposal, decide whether to bid on it, and determine the range of money to pay.

The auction starts out in rounds. Everybody puts in their first offer. As the rounds go, different publishers drop out. Finally, somebody is a winner.

In the old days of book publishing, auctions didn't exist. Auctions came in within the last thirty years. In the days of Maxwell Perkins, publishing was much more genteel. Agents dealt one on one. They would send a proposal to an editor, who would have a certain amount of time to read it and make an offer. If an agreeable offer was not made, the agent would send it to somebody else.

□ What is a floor bid in a book auction?

An editor who offers a floor bid of $50,000, for example, will get topping privileges. That is, when the last person has said "That's as high as I can go," the floor bidder is allowed the privilege of offering 10 percent or 15 percent more than the top bid. The risk is that, if nobody bid at all, that editor might have acquired the book for $10,000.

□ What is preempt?

Preempt is when an agent says to an editor, "I'll give the book to you right now for $150,000, but I want to know by the end of today if I get it."

The agent is in a dilemma. The author may be given a very healthy sum up front for the book, but might have gotten $1 million if he or she had taken it to auction. On the other hand, he or she might have gotten nothing.

□ Which books are auctioned?

Most books do not go to auction. Most are sent singly to an editor. After three weeks or four weeks—it shouldn't even be that long—the editor either buys or doesn't. If not, it goes to somebody else.

□ What are multiple submissions?

When book proposals are sent to more than one house at a time. Agents began sending multiple submissions as publishing became more competitive. It was time-consuming to send manuscripts one at a time, and multiple submissions were also a way of heating things up.

□ What are exclusives in publishing?

It's exactly what it says. An agent will say, "Because I like you and you have done well with my other books, I'll give you an exclusive on this proposal for two weeks."

□ What is positioning a book?

Positioning is identifying a book to its audience—placing it to take advantage of the market you believe is there for it.

An example would be a novel that has elements of woman in jeopardy, which is a kind of commercial fiction, but also has medical elements. How do I want to position it? Do I say it's the next Mary Higgins Clark, which is woman in jeopardy? Or do I say it's the next Robin Cook, which is medical suspense?

Positioning also has to do with announced plans. This is more hard-core positioning. Is this a big book for the house? Is the house announcing a one hundred thousand first printing and a huge ad promo? You're telling the bookseller that this is a book that the house is spending a lot of money on.

□ What are remainder sales?
It's a way of recouping money and getting rid of overstock when the life of a book is over—when it has had all the sale it's going to have in hardcover. Remainder houses buy stock that has exhausted their sales potential for a greatly reduced price. The books are sold the way you see them on remainder tables. Authors have a chance, before the book is remaindered, to buy as much of their own stock as they'd like, at a greatly reduced price.

□ What is the American Booksellers Association?
The ABA is the trade organization. American booksellers run the bookstores. There's a huge ABA meeting held every year. Publishers take booths and exhibit their newest titles. It traditionally was a way for publishers to show their upcoming list to visiting booksellers. Orders were literally placed on the convention floor. One of the complaints has been that it's become less that and just a showplace for publishers to show off their new books and lists to other publishers.

□ What is the Frankfurt Book Fair?
The Frankfurt Book Fair is the biggest international book fair. Publishers from countries all over the world come and exhibit their books. There's an American hall, a British hall, a French hall, a German hall, a Nigerian hall. It is, in essence, a rights fair. It's a chance for publishers to see what other houses are publishing all over the world and to buy the rights to those books. It's a hugely significant fair. A lot of business is done there.

□ Are there other important book fairs?
There are a lot of regional book fairs in this country. The regional ones are getting very important.

□ Do you have words of wisdom for authors in search of a publisher?
Approach the selling of your books the way you would if you were a company marketing a product.

Get an agent. I would rather always deal with an agent for many reasons. I don't have to explain the intricacies of a contract to an agent. There's an image of the rapacious editor out to skin a writer alive. The agent becomes an advocate—the author doesn't have to wonder, "Is the editor giving me the straight scoop on this?" When there's a problem with the book, I can go to the agent as a middleman and say, "Listen, these are the problems." The agent takes it one step further. The writer is getting bad news from his advocate. Rough feelings from negotiation, the point of contract, to later editorial work are avoided with an agent. Negotiation is negotiation. I'm trying to get the book for a price that I feel is reasonable, and the author wants the most money he can get. His agent and I have to do battle. It's pleasant and civil, but we're in opposite ends of the corner. If you're starting out that way with a writer, it's very hard to change gears and become the person who now says, "I'd like you change this ending; I'd like you to do this."

Everyone's book, to him or her, is original. Chances are, something like it has already been published. Pick a book in your local bookstore that is somewhat similar to yours. Who is the publisher? Write for the catalog. Would you feel comfortable having your book on that list? Is your book appropriate? Is an editor acknowledged? Send your proposal directly to him.

2

Contracts, Warranties, Indemnities, Options, Royalties, Ancillary Rights, Movie and TV Rights, and More

BRIAN DeFIORE, ASSOCIATE PUBLISHER

Hyperion
Division of Disney Book Publishing, Inc.
New York

BRIAN DeFIORE has been associate publisher at Hyperion since 1993. As an English major in college, DeFiore liked to read and wanted a job that was close to books. His first editorial jobs at St. Martin's Press served as his training ground in publishing. He went to Dell Books as senior editor and executive editor and then moved from the mass market side of the business to hardcover as executive editor and editorial director of Delacorte Press. After serving as vice president and senior editor at William Morrow, he was offered his present position.

Hyperion hired its first employee in 1990. A subsidiary of the Walt Disney Company, Hyperion was to serve as a full-service mainstream adult publisher. Hyperion Books acts as an independent publisher. "We go after authors just like HarperCollins or Random House or any other publishing house that is owned by a bigger media company," explains DeFiore. "We use Disney as clout in the marketplace, but we are not limited by the Walt Disney profile as only family entertainment."

At this writing, Hyperion publishes fifty hardcover and fifty paperback mainstream commercial books.

□ **When negotiating a contract, should an agented writer show the contract to a lawyer?**
I really don't think it's valuable to call in a lawyer. That's why agents get their 10 percent or 15 percent commission. Agents know all the publishing houses and all the publishing houses' contracts. They understand the lingo of the publishing business better than lawyers do.

□ **Why shouldn't lawyers be involved in a publishing contract? After all, contracts are what the legal profession is about.**
I've dealt with many lawyers who have been called in by their author clients. They don't understand the publishing business, they very often choose to dig in their heels on the things that an agent knows a publisher will never change, or they will spend a lot of time (which means clients' money) learning the publishing business, asking us things like, "What does a discount clause mean?"—while an agent understands.

Most starting authors will go to their family lawyer or even go to a lawyer at a big law firm to try to get them to negotiate some points on the publishing contract, which is not a contract they really understand. I don't see the value in it for a writer. There are a few lawyers who specialize in publishing contracts. There are a couple of very good publishing lawyers, whom some writers use in place of literary agents. That's a different issue and that is valuable.

□ **Do most publishers offer similar clauses and similar contracts?**
Yes. With minor changes, they're all pretty much the same.

□ **Is that a "boilerplate" contract?**
Yes. Boilerplate is the term used to indicate the publisher's standard contract. It's a word that gets bandied around a lot. It's a contract form and you fill in the blanks.

□ **Some contracts are two pages long and some are twenty-two pages long. Why?**
Some companies are more corporate than others. Some have more powerful lawyers than others. Some contracts are more rigorous than others. For the most part, they are all asking for the same things. They all set forth basically the same arrangement between the author and the publishing house on basically the same terms with some variations.

□ **The contract is offered by the publisher. How much leverage does the author have in making changes?**

Not a whole lot. That's one of the places where having an agent is very valuable in the negotiation of a contract. Most reputable agents will have dealt with that publisher in the past and will already have dealt with the difficult clauses in the publisher's contract. If an unagented author is offered a contract by Random House or some big publisher and they send a blank form contract, the author has very little leverage to get any changes into that contract. However, if that same author has a great big powerful agent who, in the last six months, has negotiated ten other $1 million contracts with Random House in which he had leverage over the publisher because the publisher wanted those authors so badly, that agent knows where the publishing house will be flexible in its contract and will often be able to get those same terms into a contract for any of his clients.

□ **What are the areas of the contract where the author does have leverage to make changes?**

Numbers of copies of free books to the author are easy to negotiate. Royalty rates are more standard. There is a basic standard in book publishing—hardcover is 10 percent on the first 5,000, 12.5 percent on the next 5,000, and 15 percent thereafter. Mass market is usually 8 percent to 150,000 and 10 percent thereafter. Trade paperback is usually a straight 7 percent.

□ **Does that change with the second book published?**

Not as much as it changes with a successful book.

□ **What about other rights, such as book clubs, movie, TV, and foreign rights?**

Often the publishers get all of those rights because the publisher has subsidiary rights departments that can sell those rights effectively—certainly more effectively than an author can from his or her living room.

If an author is represented by a powerful agent, like ICM or William Morris, which have their own film divisions, then the agent will usually hold on to film and performance and many of the other rights—as many as they can.

Book club rights are always part of the publisher's deal. The publisher always sells book club rights and paperback rights. Usually the agent will hold on to serial rights and movie and TV and foreign rights.

Foreign rights are something the publisher will pay extra for and negotiate to get.

□ **Do most contracts have the option clause of first refusal of the author's next book?**

Almost always. The process of publishing a book is really the process of helping build an author's career. It depends on what sort of book we're talking about.

Certainly, in fiction publishing what a publisher is doing, in publishing the book, is not only publishing the subject that the book is about, but is also publishing the author, trying to get recognition for the author. In doing so, the publisher often spends a lot of money to try to get the bookstores and the media to pay attention to this author and this author's name. In return for that, I think it's fair that the publisher at least gets a chance to read that author's next book first and make an offer for it or not. Those option clauses rarely have any lock-in price. It's just a way that the publisher gets to look first, rather than being put in a position of either not even having a chance for the next book or being put in a competitive situation for the next book.

□ **Does that mean that if the publisher likes the book, it's his?**
No. It means if the publisher likes the book, he can make an offer for it. I get to read it first and negotiate with the author first before she or he sends it off and shows it to other publishers. It means that the publisher is getting the right to not have to compete with every other publisher in town in the first instance, if they can come to terms with the author. If they can't come to terms with the author, the author can, almost always, do what he or she wants.

□ **Are there other elements of the book contract that the author should understand?**
Copyright is standard. It's almost always held by the author. And it should be. Libel is standard. An author will very rarely be able to change. Publishers are very legal, very corporate. The basic premise is the same in every publisher's contract, which authors may not like, but authors are responsible for what they say in their books. Authors must be certain that what they deliver to a publisher does not libel and does not infringe on anybody's rights and does not break any laws.

□ **What do most contracts say with regard to libel or plagiarism?**
Most publishing contracts have a warranty and indemnity clause. The warranty part of it says something like, "I, the author, promise to you, the publisher, that this manuscript does not libel anyone, does not break any laws, will not get anyone in trouble"—all the legal things that it won't do. It also says, "I am the author of this book, I am the only author of this book, I did not plagiarize anyone, I did not use anyone else's material without permission." That sort of thing.

The indemnity portion says, "If that's not true, and it turns out in court that I have broken the law or I did not have the right to sell you this, then you, the publisher, are held harmless and I am responsible for any legal repercussions that come up through the publishing of this book."

☐ **Does the publisher usually stand by the author?**
The publisher almost always stands by the author, financially too. What usually happens in reality is when a publishing house and an author are sued, the publishing house goes to court and the publishing house pays for the legal fees. If it is found in court that the author was responsible, that the author did knowingly break the law, the publisher will often try to get its money back from the author.

☐ **When an agented author is offered a book contract, must he or she personally negotiate the contract with the agent and the editor?**
No. The agent doesn't even come here. It's almost always all done over the telephone.

☐ **How are advances determined?**
[An advance is money provided from the publisher to the author before the completion of a book.]
    It all depends on the ultimate sales potential of a book. Obviously, if we're talking about a seven-figure advance, it's a book that the publisher believes has enormous sales potential, either because the writer already has published successful books and has a built-in readership, or is some sort of expert or celebrity in the field, who the publisher believes has built-in name recognition. The amount a publisher pays is a function of (1) how many books they think they can sell, which gives them the amount they're able to spend, and (2) the amount they *have to* spend, because, like everyone, the publisher tries to acquire the property for as little risk as possible.

☐ **How is the first printing determined?**
The same way. It can be anywhere from five thousand copies to a million copies.

☐ **What is the standard author's deadline for a manuscript completion?**
That also varies enormously, from a month to five years—five years is pretty rare. I've been involved with books where the deadline is years. A certain type of serious biography in which the author is going to have to take two or three years for the research would warrant a longer deadline. The usual term for delivery in a contract is a year. However, if it looks like the author has been working, the work has progressed, and the author can show the publisher some of the material that has been done in that year and it's good, the publisher will almost always give an extension on that deadline. If, however, in that year the author has not come up with anything that is publishable and the material is out of control and the writer doesn't look like he's going to be able to deliver it any time soon, the publisher may cancel the contract and ask for the advance back.

□ **What if you receive a manuscript that isn't what you want? What if, on paper, it fits the bill, but it's just not acceptable to you?**
Every publishing contract has a clause that says something like, "The manuscript must be delivered in form and content acceptable to the publisher."

□ **Isn't that somewhat subjective?**
It's completely subjective. However, an author really is protected from the publisher just changing their mind. In almost every instance, when a publisher buys a book, they buy on the basis of a partial manuscript or a proposal, which tells exactly what the book is going to be, what the style of the book is going to be, with some sample writing material that allows the publisher to see what the author is capable of. If, in fact, the author delivers ostensibly the book that was promised in the proposal, the publisher can't say, "I've changed my mind and want a different book."

The issue more often comes up when the writer goes off track and changes what he or she thought the book was going to be and the book has a different editorial slant from what was presented in the proposal. Even so, when the manuscript is delivered, a court of law has determined that a publisher has to demonstrate that they have given a writer editorial guidance along the way, has read the manuscript, and has given the author a chance to fix it to the publisher's satisfaction. Most publishing contracts have clauses that say if the manuscript is unacceptable, the publisher will tell the author why it's unacceptable and give him or her a period of time to fix it. A publisher can't just say, "Gee, I've changed my mind. Give me my money back."

□ **Do you have words to the wise for authors in negotiating a contract?**
Get an agent. Even if a publishing house has offered you a contract, at that point it's wise to call an agent and say, "Would you take over this negotiation?" The agent can be very helpful. If you get to the point where you're offered a contract by a publisher, it will be very easy to find an agent. The hard part of an agent's job is making a sale. Once the sale is made, agents can negotiate the contract in a snap. That's what they are trained to do. I really do think it's very valuable for a writer to have an agent.

3

"The Big Push" High-Concept Books, Creating Blockbusters, Underappreciated Aspects of Getting a Book on the Best-Seller List, and More

RICK HORGAN, EXECUTIVE EDITOR

HarperCollins Publishers
New York

RICK HORGAN has been executive editor at HarperCollins since December 1992. As a college English major, he had vague ideas about what he wanted to do. After a six-week crash course in publishing, he was instantly turned on to becoming an editor. Horgan landed a job at the Scott Meredith Literary Agency, worked for a short time in the technical, scholarly side of publishing, and in 1984 took a position with Donald Fine, Inc. At the beginning with this small start-up company, which blossomed into a midsize publisher within a few years, he acquired fiction, including three best-selling thrillers by Dale Brown and *Indecent Proposal* by Jack Engelhard, basis of the hit movie starring Robert Redford.

Horgan went to Warner Books in 1988, where his first book, *Leadership Secrets of Attila the Hun,* sold two hundred thousand hardcover copies and five hundred thousand copies in trade paperback, and became the tenth best-selling nonfiction title of 1989.

After five years at Warner Books, Horgan accepted his present position as executive editor at HarperCollins (in December 1992), where he is editor to Jeffrey Archer, Dan Quayle, Dennis Byrd, and other celebrity authors.

HarperCollins, one of the largest publishing companies in the world, is also one of the oldest (180 years). It published Charles Dickens and Herman Melville. HarperCollins publishes 150 hardcover and trade paperbacks each season. In the trade division, HarperCollins has twenty editors, who see approximately twenty thousand proposals a year. "I've heard," says Horgan, "that industry-wide at any given time there are on editors' desks or in the mail thirty thousand proposals or projects."

□ **How do you deal with the number of proposals (20–25) you typically see a week?**
It can be suffocating. It can exhaust every hour of your day. As a defensive mechanism, virtually every house has ceased to look at slush material and unsolicited submissions. At some houses, such as ours, there's a token effort to give slush submissions a cursory look. Junior-level assistants convene every Friday and go through the slush that has accumulated that week. That is a one-hour meeting and I would guess that half of it is given over to gossip and shop talk. That leaves a half-hour to make a judgment call on probably one hundred submissions. What they're really looking for is the letter or proposal that has been misrouted—the *New York Times* best-selling author who, for some unexplainable reason, mailed a letter of inquiry to the editorial department and not to a specific editor.

That's not to say if someone in that meeting spots something that they have an intense interest in they might not take it out of the meeting and spend a few days looking at it. In most cases, though, there's a yea or nay decision made right there.

□ **How do you deal with writers who send you proposals because you're a friend, a relative, or a friend of a friend?**
The bane of my existence is manuscripts that come to me from nephews, aunts, uncles, friends of friends, and so on. Although I have the best of intentions, inevitably I leave this manuscript on the shelf for six months before overwhelming guilt finally drives me to make a snap-judgment call on it.

□ **Why is an editor's work life so frenetic?**
It's because you spend so much of your time building relationships with agents—agents who have clout. You take them to lunch, you spend a lot of money, you're on the phone with them. You're constantly following up, trying to see things. When those manuscripts accumulate on your desk, they scream out "priority." When I know I have on my desk a novel that Robert Gottlieb at the William

Morris Agency just sent me or a nonfiction proposal from Binky Urban at International Creative Management, I find it impossible to look at that novel from Uncle Fred. I find it impossible to go down to the bookstore and pick up something that was well reviewed, that I have a casual interest in, so I can take it home with me or read it on the train. I really feel that burden of getting through this material that agents send me and responding in a prompt fashion.

The whole pace of the business has accelerated. It used to be this gentlemanly process. Fifty years ago there were no multiple submissions. Agents—and there weren't as many agents as there are today—would submit a manuscript to one editor, wait for that editor to make a decision, and then go to the next editor. That is not the case these days. These days twenty manuscripts go out on a given day, and the agent will usually call to hype you on it, to tell you about all the movie interest, and so on. "And I expect this one to go fast," he'll warn me.

□ **What is the effect of the agent's hype?**
What that does is create a feeding frenzy. Everyone feels compelled to read the thing within twenty-four hours or within forty-eight hours. In the case of the proposals that seem hot, no one respects the closing date. I'll get something on September 1 that will have a closing date of September 28 and I know, if the agent calls me twice to hype me on this, if he's saying it will go fast, I know that I have to get my act together. I have to look at this thing, certainly within forty-eight hours. I know that other houses will have been calling and putting money on the table by then.

It creates constant ripples of panic. Something that just came to me two days ago suddenly has megaoffers. That's the nature of the beast these days.

One of the reasons this situation exists is because the whole industry has become blockbuster oriented. Everyone is looking for those titles that they can blow out, and they're willing to overpay for them.

Woe to that editor who let the submission languish in the pile only to read in *Publishers Weekly* next week that nine houses were involved in an auction for it and it went for $2 million.

□ **Will you talk about the underappreciated aspects of getting a book on the best-seller list? Waving your pom-poms? Knowing how to get people at a major company like HarperCollins to focus on your book?**
I think the big myth in this business is that quality will win out, that cream will rise to the top. It's a misconception that I labored under when I was first getting into the business. The first novel that I edited, I thought, "If I invoke the spirit of Max Perkins, roll up my sleeves, and apply myself, I can transform it into something that is wonderful and some sort of spontaneous process will occur once it reaches the shelf. It will be recognized."

What I learned is that the whole industry is driven by what I call The Big Push. Every publishing house sits down a few months prior to the publication of its next list and makes a decision about which books should get The Big Push. Very often it's the books that they pay the most money for. For that reason, agents have a valid argument when they say, "An advance is an advance, and there is going to be back-end money, but the fact is, the more money you pay for this up front, the better job you'll do for it." It's hard to counter that argument because, in fact, that's the case.

□ How do you determine which books will get The Big Push?

Each season when we get together, we look at, say, 150 titles in that list. There's a finite amount of advertising and promotion money that can be allocated to these titles. The top twenty-five titles, in terms of the amount that is spent on them, are usually those that are given The Big Push. Occasionally there are titles that different people argue were actually "a steal, they really have quite a bit of potential, we really should get behind them."

Of the handful of great books published in a given year, I'd say that 25 percent of them are perceived as such by publishing houses and will get that sort of support.

Another 5 percent will get a belated Big Push. A book like *The Bridges of Madison County* is a book that really didn't get The Big Push early on. It got an after-the-fact Big Push. It was a case of word of mouth driving the sales where it showed up on the publisher's radar screen. Once that happened, money was found, more advertising occurred, and so on.

□ What about the books that don't get The Big Push?

The difference between the book that gets the Push and the book that doesn't is stark, it's unbelievable.

The book that doesn't receive that type of support gets a review mailing. One hundred and fifty copies of the book are sent to reviewers across the United States with a press release.

□ What is done for the books that get The Big Push?

Those books get a full-page ad in the *New York Times*. Preprints or bound galleys are usually created and used to whet interest and to create a buzz. Those books will have radio spots. They'll probably have a publicity tour, if the authors are at all telegenic or mediagenic. There will be complimentary mailings of the books to movers and shakers. They'll probably get book club selections. They'll probably have a lot of money lavished on the cover—you'll see an embossing and foil. They'll probably have counter displays; perhaps special discounts will be offered to get the book into the bookstores in quantity.

The publisher may have worked out an arrangement with one of the big chains like Barnes & Noble, Walden, or Crown to actually buy real estate in the store. The way that works, practically speaking, is that a chain comes up with a program. If your title is selected for that program, it receives prominent display in the front of the store. The publisher pays a fee to get the book in the store window.

□ **What other factors are involved in creating a blockbuster?**

The other thing—and all of this is leading up to the pom-poms—which must be considered is that the chains have initiated something that has spread to all of the independent booksellers. All sales are now tracked on computer, which means that when a first novel is distributed, it has its first record of sale. It has its net sale level and its level of returns. When the rep goes to sell the author's next book, he has to work off that history. As soon as he mentions the title, the bookseller keys it into the computer to see how the first book did. If he sees for a hardcover, for instance, that the net sale was below 50 percent, or below 65 percent even, he is going to be extremely skeptical. He will probably take fewer copies than he did the first time around. If the rep goes into the store the third time, and the net sale on the first two books was poor, he may not get *any* copies of the book into that account. This situation puts tremendous pressure on an editor and, of course, on the author to make that first book work. It's either an upward track for that author, or it's a nontrack. That's different from the way it used to be. A decade ago, the industry showed a great deal of patience toward authors such as Ann Tyler, Elmore Leonard, and Tony Hillerman—people who would publish eight or ten books before they broke out. The industry is not that forgiving anymore. You have to make that first book work. Thus, the need for the editor to make that book the one that gets The Big Push.

□ **How do you convince the house that first book will be a blockbuster if given The Big Push?**

It's incumbent on the editor. The editor obviously believes in all of his books. The editor obviously believes that all of his books deserve The Big Push. That's the task that the editor sets for himself in convincing the house that this book, regardless of whether he paid $1 million or $10,000 for it, deserves The Big Push.

There are all sorts of tricks that an editor can perform. I would emphasize the difference between an editor who is trying to create this perception within the house and an editor who is just putting the manuscript into production. The difference is a hundredfold in terms of the book's ultimate prospects. It's a whole different mind-set.

□ **What "tricks" can an editor perform to create the perception within the company that a given book is big?**

The editor who wants to create this perception can do a lot of things. When the book is acquired, he can send around a memo thanking everyone for their support. Sort of ballyhooing that we have this thing. He can immediately type up a summary of the book and get it into the hands of the right people, who are talking with foreign accounts all of the time, who may be attending the ABA convention or the Frankfurt Book Fair and will want to talk it up. He obviously has to attend to the editorial details, make sure all of the wrinkles are smoothed out. He has to do that hard work.

Once the manuscript comes in, he has to validate it. The way he validates it is by getting blurbs. There's a lazy man's way of getting blurbs and there's the pulling-your-hair-out way. The lazy man's way is to ask the author if he knows anyone. If the author doesn't know anyone, the job is finished. The other way is for an editor to spend three days of his life trying to come up with names and addresses. If you're editing a thriller about kite flying, you go into the bookstore and look in the fiction section for thrillers that deal with this subject, even tangentially. You try to find out who the author's agent is, or where the author lives, you inspect the bio, and you get the address. You sit down and write these authors a personal letter, and ask them, "Please, please, please, will you look at this book, and will you give me a quote?" And, hopefully, you get these early comments in time to persuade other people in the house to think, "Hey, we have something here, here's this book we bought maybe for only $10,000, but suddenly there's this river of quotes that seems to be washing over us." Talk about reinforcement! If you're a marketing department head and you get a memo in your in-box every three days about a given book, pretty soon it's subliminal. There is that perception: "Hey, this is a book we should get behind."

There are other tricks. If you can weave a story around the author's background, you can give it mythic proportion. That can become a handle that everyone in the whole organization can use to sell the book. We're all aware of *Confederacy of Dunces* by John Kennedy Toole, who committed suicide, and the way the house leveraged that whole story. Editors are always trying to discover the unique aspect of an author's background that will tweak the reader's interest.

□ **What other editorial tasks make a difference to the success of a book?**

All along the way there are obligatory tasks that can be handled in a standard way or in a way that is really thoughtful. The flap copy (jacket copy) of a book is extraordinarily important. The publicity release is extraordinarily important. The art department is frequently the busiest department at a publishing company. Sometimes the deadlines that department has to contend with are excruciating. In a situation like that, the effort that is made can be pro forma. If you allow that to happen, if you don't strongly object, strongly advocate that the designer go back and take a second look, it can be dooming, literally dooming the book to a nonsale, particularly in the case of a paperback.

It's important to have something on the cover that depicts what the book is about. I've seen a lot of books go in the bookstores that have interesting colors, interesting type, a lot of silver and a lot of gold, but the cover doesn't say anything. If you're a browser and you don't see anything on the spine, any kind of illustration or image, anything that suggests what this book is about, I think that's a handicap.

□ Do authors have input?

The smart author does, such as James Grady (author of *Six Days of the Condor*), who has been in the business a while and has suffered enough slings and arrows. He will send a letter a few weeks after he has sent the manuscript telling me all the things I should be doing. I don't mind that because it's a reminder, something to jog my memory.

Most authors won't do that. Most leave this task up to the publisher. They assume editors are the experts. The author has to realize that the squeaky wheel gets the grease. It's a tightrope that the author has to walk because the difference between being a gentle, constructive nudger and poisoning the atmosphere is razor-thin. I've seen it get out of control. That first memo from the author, with eight suggestions for what we can do for the book, was appreciated, but by the time we get the fifth memo and the twelfth phone call, suddenly everyone in the house has turned against that author. He has become a headache.

If you're an author, the most important thing is to not take anything for granted, to ask to be part of the process to the degree that you can look at things. "Can I see the publicity release? Can I see the flap copy? Can I look at the design of the book? Do you have a rough sketch of the jacket?" Those sorts of things will head off disaster.

□ Will you do those things for the author, if he asks?

Usually I will.

Authors who have clout will usually write into the contract that they have approval of the jacket, a lot of other things. But the first-time author is usually not in a position to demand that.

□ Tell me other secrets that can help a book get priority.

Ask yourself this question: Can the book can be summed up in a single sentence? That is extremely important. I have this phrase I throw around all the time that's also thrown around in Hollywood: high concept. I'm talking about an idea that can be summed up in a single sentence, that's easily explainable. Producers love high-concept movies. Publishers love high-concept books.

☐ **Why do publishers love high-concept books?**
It's the nature of the process. A chain is set up. One person sells the book to the next person, who sells the book to the next person. The editor sells the book to the editorial board, the publisher sells the book to the rep, the rep sells the book to the bookseller, the bookseller sells the book to the consumer. There's not a lot of time for this. When a rep goes into a bookstore, if he has 150 titles to sell and he has a half-hour meeting or an hour meeting with that account, how much time can he spend on a single book? If you've written a first novel that requires a paragraph of explanation to really understand, you're going to be at a disadvantage.

☐ **What other advice would you give authors?**
Use your imagination and don't fall back on something that you've seen on TV. It's one of the most common reasons for rejecting things—that they're derivative.

Writers should never attempt to write a book in a genre that they're not intimately familiar with. It is disaster to write a science fiction novel or mystery novel without having read most of what's out there. Because, again, you run that risk of exploiting the same idea that twelve other people have exploited.

If you're pitching something, even if you're pitching it to an agent, it's always useful to compare what you've written to another book. It's like this or it's like that. That's giving the agent his handle, which is giving the editor the handle, which is giving everyone down the line their handle for the book.

Think about the demographics of the book. Think about the audience. This applies to nonfiction as well as fiction. If your approach is narrowing the audience for the topic, if you're writing a book that's only going to be read by gay males over the age of fifty, that book is less attractive than a book that is going to appeal to men, to women, to people of all ages.

4

Successful Fiction and Other Philosophies of Publishing

The Editor of *The Bridges of Madison County* Tells the Story of Her Excellent Discovery

MAUREEN EGEN, VICE PRESIDENT

Warner Books

New York

MAUREEN EGEN began her career at Doubleday as editorial director of science publishing, was promoted to associate editorial director of Anchor Press, a division of Doubleday, and then became editorial director of the Doubleday Book Clubs, where she stayed for eleven years before joining Warner Books. She has been vice president of Warner Books and publisher of Warner hardcover books since September 1990.

Warner Books, a division of Time-Warner, Inc., publishes fiction and nonfiction. Egen claims that Warner Books is a relatively small house. "We have a big name because we are a very commercial house," she says. Warner publishes 50 to 60 hardcover books a year and about 200 to 250 paperbacks for mass market and trade.

According to Egen, Warner's list includes books that will be instant best-sellers or are written by authors they are grooming to be best-selling authors. "We are very promotion driven," says Egen. "The books that we publish are primarily by well-known people. I can't say authors, exactly, because in many cases they aren't authors. They're celebrities, who are now becoming authors. We do best here with books that are by people who are themselves highly promotable."

Egen's discovery, *The Bridges of Madison County*, is a 171-page romantic novel by Robert James Waller. It has topped the charts as the best-selling fiction hardcover book of all time, with sales of over five million copies.

□ **How did you discover** *The Bridges of Madison County?*
I had just come to Warner from The Literary Guild, where I was publisher and editorial director of all the Doubleday Clubs. I'd been here two months. I went to have lunch with an old friend, Aaron Priest, an agent in New York who has a very small agency but a number of prominent authors, including Erma Bombeck. We were sitting there talking and I said, "Now you're supposed to sell me a book."

He said, "I really don't have much at the moment, but there is one little thing that I read and a couple of people here read and some of us really like this a lot, but we don't really know what to do with it. It's fiction and it's a story about a photographer who spends four days in Iowa and falls in love and has to leave."

And I said, "It sounds really wonderful. I'd like to read it." So he sent it over. I read it quickly, because it's very short, and I bought it. It was the first book I bought for Warner.

□ **How did Robert Waller fit into Warner's requirement for "well-known people who are highly promotable"?**
Robert Waller turned out to be more than we expected when we bought the book. He turned out to be a highly promotable author. We bought the book because we really believed it was different and special.

□ **What is your theory about successful fiction?**
My theory is that there are many, many people out there who write, who have other full-time, so-called day jobs. And they're able, in their writing, to bring a view that someone who stays locked in a room all the time cannot bring to a book.

□ **What are you saying to writers with your anecdote about** *Bridges?*
I'd say to use what you know. Don't try to make it all up. Robert James Waller, the author of *Bridges,* was a professor of business, who had written all of his adult life. He is also a musician. Waller has his Ph.D. in economics, was a full-time professor and, in fact, was the dean of the business school at the university at which he taught in Iowa.

He's also a published photographer, so he brought a lot of know-how to *Bridges*. He knew what a photographer would do. He knew what kind of lenses, what kind of film, what kind of light to expect or not expect or want or not get or whatever. So he was able to bring a lot of information that someone who is just sitting in a quiet little room can't.

□ What do you look for in an author?

I really like working with writers who write out of a compulsion to write, but do it with a mind and a set of emotions that are shaped and formed by the rest of the world and by some other existence. They can bring something different, something special to a book.

□ Do you have other words of wisdom for authors?

I think that the only way someone becomes a published writer is by writing, writing, writing—writing all the time, and finding whatever outlets one can find in which to be published. Whether it's short stories, or literary journals, or pieces for your local newspaper, you've got to just keep writing, writing, writing.

The second point is to write about what you know about.

The third is to remember whom you're writing for. It's really hard to say this to writers, because they don't believe they should be writing for anyone but themselves. But in fact, if you want to be published—the idea of publishing is to broadcast the written word. That means that you have to be writing in a way that other people want to hear. If you want an audience, you have to aim for an audience. You have to know who they are. You don't necessarily have to know what they want to hear, but you have to feel that you're talking to someone and not just yourself and your PC.

5

Publishing: The Present and the Future

CHARLES CONRAD, EXECUTIVE EDITOR

Anchor Books
Imprint of Doubleday
Division of Bantam Doubleday Dell Publishing Group
New York

CHARLES CONRAD, Executive Editor of Anchor Books, was an English major in college. After graduation, he attended a publishing institute in Denver. In 1984 he joined the editorial department of New American Library. After a year, he went to Newmarket Press, a company known for movie tie-in books, then to Warner Books. In 1991 he accepted a position as senior editor at Anchor Books, where he later became executive editor. His editing specialties are current affairs, popular culture, and social issues.

Anchor Books, a division of Doubleday, was founded in the early 1950s by Jason Epstein, now the vice president and editorial director of Random House. Anchor was the first publisher of trade paperback books—academically oriented paperbacks for a mainstream audience. The company presently publishes sixty books a year. According to Conrad, Anchor's strongest areas are black history, black issues, women's studies, social issues, popular culture, and multicultural fiction.

Anchor receives about five or six proposals for original books and another half-dozen slush proposals each day. "We look at those," says Conrad. "Writers are smarter these days, sending proposals to specific editors."

□ Has publishing changed?
Publishing has changed a lot in the last decade. There's been an increasing bottom-line orientation, which can work both for and against authors.

□ How can this bottom line orientation work for authors?
If an author submits something that's even slightly original and it's well done, well proposed, and well written, publishers will take it very seriously. More often these days, interesting and original books seem to come from unknown and first-time authors.

□ How can it work against authors?
There's an increasing emphasis on the tried and true, subjects and authors that have worked before, so that can work against new writers. Part of the reason for this quick hit mentality is that publishers' costs have been cut back and there are fewer publishers than there were ten years ago.

□ How has publishing changed in terms of new technologies?
There are more possibilities for developing books from just the book form into various electronic media. Every major company has a new media division set up to develop CD-ROMs, on-line products, and computer disk products from the things that the corporation does—books, records, videos, and so forth.

□ What is CD-ROM?
It's like a compact disk that can accommodate everything from still photos to video to audio to text. It's often interactive, allowing you to access various kinds of information randomly, the way you want to, just as you can page through a book.

□ What should writers do to deal with the new media?
They should be aware of the various media and how their work could be translated into another medium. For example, if they're writing a book about country music, they should think about how it could be translated into a CD-ROM that would include a video of a country music performer, audio of their songs, and text talking about their background.

Writers are already involved in writing their books on computers and using computers to access information. By writing their books on computers, they're digitizing information. Once that's done, many things can be done with that information.

Authors should think about this from the beginning because that's going to be the trend.

□ Are there differences between fiction and nonfiction in this technology?
Yes, and not only between fiction and nonfiction, but in the kinds of nonfiction that are compatible. Anything that's got a reference or a browse format is much

more compatible to the electronic media. I can't see how people would want to read novels on a computer screen.

A good example might be movie guidebooks for movies on TV and video. There's no reason why those books should be printed every nine months. They could easily be put on a disk. You could get an update to stick in your computer. There is going to be competition for those in the future.

□ **Have you had proposals that were applicable for the new media?**
Yes. For example, we recently received a proposal for a financial guide. There was a lot of interest in it as a book. Our new media person thought it was a great idea. We're making an offer on it both as a book and as a CD-ROM.

□ **How does the new media affect an author in negotiating a contract?**
Agents, these days, are very careful to define the various electronic media. There used to be a clause in the contract that said "electronic rights," but no one knew what that meant. Agents are now careful to designate whether it means CD-ROM, on-line distribution, and the like.

□ **Is there a significant market for electronic publishing at this time and what about the future and the new technologies?**
I'm not sure there is at this stage. I read a story in *The New Yorker* about Bill Gates and Microsoft. He describes a box on your TV, that's now just your cable switcher box, but will become like a little computer terminal, allowing you to access many things beyond cable channels. When that happens, it will be much more pervasive because everybody's got a TV and a cable box, but not everybody has a computer. It won't be long before you can order any movie you want from your video store and watch any time you want. You can already watch pay per view, but it's somewhat limited.

□ **Are publishers now preparing for the future, in terms of CD-ROM, on-line, and the like?**
Yes. But I think a lot of the things coming out now are. I don't want to say experimental, but they're first generation. The technology will eventually catch up and become refined enough to be used on a widespread basis.

□ **Do you have advice for authors in search of a publisher in light of these changes?**
Publishers will look very favorably on authors who are knowledgeable about how their work can be translated into an electronic medium. If I received a proposal that was good as a book and the author also showed me how he or she thought that it could work as a CD-ROM, it would be a plus, something in the writer's favor, two selling points for the book.

6

New Media and Book Publishing

JONATHAN GUTTENBERG, DIRECTOR
OF NEW MEDIA
Bantam Doubleday Dell Publishing Group
New York

JONATHAN GUTTENBERG, Director of New Media at Bantam Doubleday Dell, has always been involved with computers. Before college, he consulted and ran his own software company. His college major was communications with a minor in marketing. A class called "New Directions in Telecommunications" was a turning point for him. After graduation, Guttenberg worked in corporate development at Columbia Pictures and at Viacom, where he ultimately became involved in interactive media. He worked on the creation of Viacom New Media, Viacom International's interactive publishing unit. He then worked in Viacom New Media, first as director of business development and operations, then as director of marketing. In October 1993 he went to Bantam Doubleday Dell, where he started their new media group.

Bantam Doubleday Dell is the second largest trade book publisher in the United States. It is the U.S. book publishing arm of Bertelsmann AG, a broad-based, privately held German media company.

☐ **What does your job entail?**
My job is to create a new media group within a traditional book publisher. That involves tracking the development of new technologies that affect our core business and determining what are the best ways for a traditional book publisher to leverage its core strengths within the businesses that emerge out of these new technologies.

□ What is new media?

It is the digital delivery of content. Rather than appearing on a printed page, content appears in some other shape or form—on a piece of physical media, such as a floppy disk or a compact disc, or delivered over the same wires that deliver either telephone or cable television, or over the air. The content is displayed on a wide range of devices, ranging from a personal computer to a television set to a handheld device to a virtual reality helmet.

We're very much in the early days of a new medium. Many of the early products are results of people translating products from an existing medium to a new medium. In many cases these first products take limited advantage of what these new media can afford us. Some of these early products work for their audience; many do not. The market is somewhat forgiving early-on since consumers are hungry for product. However, as the market matures, it becomes much more competitive and there is less room for product that does not deliver significant value to the consumer. The problem is that we have not yet fully learned the language of this new medium. Words written for the film are entirely different than those written for the stage or for a book. While the letters are the same and the words are the same, the way they're put together to impart ideas or tell a story are entirely different. To make matters worse, with new media we are not talking about just one type of media. We're still just learning the storytelling devices that are going to be used in the new medium. We're learning every day. Each new product gives everyone the ability to decide what worked and what didn't work. Other companies often incorporate and refine these new storytelling devices into their future products.

We view new media as simply another format, similar to the way that the paperback or audio are other formats in which a book may appear.

□ How are you setting up your new media efforts?

We're setting ourselves up to integrate seamlessly with Bantam Doubleday Dell's current publishing operation.

□ What does new media offer that you can't currently do on a printed page?

It would be impossible to create a complete list of all of the things that you can do in many cases because we are still learning. What you can do depends on the device you are using and on what medium the material is delivered. For example, you can include animation and video. You can also offer new ways in which to view the material. Instead of going through the book in a linear fashion, an interactive product can allow you to search quickly for different sections. When viewing information on basketball you can jump to a video on basketball or to a biography of Michael Jordan. You can also allow the viewer to make choices in the narrative—does the protagonist go left and enter the house, or right and jump into the pool—that ultimately affect the ending. In addition, new media can allow you to interact with other people to share what each person thought of the story.

□ What is the difference between new media publishing and traditional book publishing?

In traditional book publishing you start with the author and you finish with a manuscript that eventually ends up in bookstores. With a new media title, you start with an author and you end up with a piece of physical media or something that's distributed over a network, either over a wire such as through your telephone line or over the air. With an electronic property, we usually involve another company or another group. That group is known as a developer. A developer has a variety of different skills needed to produce an interactive property. In some cases that group may reside within a publishing company and in other cases they may be an outside company contracted for a particular project.

□ What skills do developers offer to produce an interactive property?

The developer writes the instructions that tell the machine where things should go, how they should look, such that at the end of the day we have a final product. The skills needed by a developer depend on the final form of the product. The skills may include writing, animation, video production, computer programming, and/or interface design. Interface design is analogous to page layout in a book except that it refers to what the screen looks like and how someone gets through the product.

□ What is the role of the author?

The author is usually the originator of the idea. Much like a film, the author may decide to be involved in the process or may decide not to be involved. In some cases, the author will write the screenplay. In other cases, the author will not. Similarly, for an interactive project, there are a variety of levels of involvement. It depends on the author and the skills that the author brings to the table as well as his or her interest.

□ Do you expect people to read entire books on a computer screen?

It's not the place that most people want to read books. Unless a computer offers added value that is appropriate to the specific book, most people would prefer to read it on a printed page. The eye strain involved reading text on a computer screen is significant. Also, it's not easy to curl up in bed with your computer.

We might expect people to read segments of books. One company found that the most that anyone really wanted to read on a screen was two screens. It's important to note that the average screen displays significantly less text than the average printed page.

Screen technology will get better. As technology gets better, people may be able to spend longer times reading off computer screens. Ultimately what will develop are handheld devices that are used for reading text. These will, however, only be successful if they are as easy to read as a book—both in terms of the quality of the text on the screen and the ease of use of the device itself. From the reader's standpoint these should offer significant value since you will be able to carry several books at once in something that takes the space of a paperback book. Books distributed in this manner will also help the environment.

□ How much progress has been made with the new media?

We have probably more unanswered questions than answered questions. We haven't seen the tip of the iceberg yet. Many people have taken different stabs at this. However, it will be a matter of time before we learn exactly what the consumer wants.

Almost all of the major publishers have an in-house group that is responsible for new media.

One of our plans is to figure out the position we as a company should take now and in the future. We need to focus on some means for our authors to benefit from these new markets. We're exploring products that are straight implementations of the original text as well as derivative properties that are based on the characters, the worlds, and the stories that the author originally created, and trying to translate those into new media products.

□ How can new media help an author of "real" books?

In the not too distant future, consumers' first exposure to an author may be through a new media title. That exposure may motivate them to read other books that the author has written, as well as the original book that the new media product is based on.

We've seen interactive encyclopedias, which allow users to find information and see relationships between information that they couldn't easily view in the printed form.

□ Will authors earn more from new media versions of their books, as they do when movie rights are bought?

Yes. It represents another source of potential revenue for the author.

□ How are publishers affected by the new media?

It is becoming increasingly important for publishers to maintain an author's work in electronic form. That's not happening overnight. In addition, many new media products require an additional investment of capital by the publisher that is significantly more than converting a hardcover book into a paperback.

□ Will publishers incorporate computers into the production process?
Publishers must figure out how to maintain information in digital form throughout the production process. Publishing companies are continually looking at how to refine their production process. The incorporation of computers into that flow will help reduce time and increase efficiency.

We're starting to see more and more interest in computers. Computers are finding their way into more and more people's homes. One study indicated that as of November 1993, before the prime Christmas selling season, roughly 50 percent of households with kids had computers.

People are becoming familiar with computers in the workplace and in schools. The prices of computers are dropping. Also, the functionality of computers is continuing to increase—computers are becoming faster every year, but without a subsequent rise in price. A computer that you can buy today for $800 would probably have cost $3,000 two years ago. That $800 computer is significantly more powerful than the two-year-old $3,000 computer.

CD-ROM is another reason. With CD-ROM, a program is put on a compact disc, which looks the same as a regular audio compact disc. The difference between a floppy disc and a compact disc is that a compact disc can hold as much information as 650 floppy disks.

□ How many CD-ROM drives are presently installed in people's homes?
At the end of 1993 there were over two million CD-ROM drives in people's homes. That number is expected to double in 1994.

□ Will writers, editors, and agents who are not computer literate survive in publishing?
Yes. As we go back to our movie example, an author does not necessarily need to be film literate to have his or her book realized as a motion picture. It's similar here. Also, like movies, not every book will translate into a new media product.

□ How will new media affect books as we now know them?
Books aren't going away. Instead, new media offers new ways to reach our market.

New media is a different type of experience. When people are using multimedia, it may be at the expense of reading books. But, as I said before, this will also have the effect of exposing people to an author's work and may encourage them to explore further other books that the author has written.

□ What are other trends in new media?

On-line services is another growing area. The three largest commercial services are Prodigy, CompuServe, and America On-line. Internet, which many people talk about, is a government-operated service that links many privately held computers and university- and government-held computers.

Again, while I don't expect people to read books delivered via on-line services to their computers, these services will allow people to see books presented in different ways or to read excerpts of books that will tempt them into reading the whole book.

On-line services will also offer people a way to communicate after they've read a book. People will be able to find other people who have read the same books, so they can talk about whether they liked it or didn't like it, or discuss the ending.

□ Like book clubs on-line?

Exactly.

□ How can on-line services affect authors in promoting their books?

Some publishing companies use on-line services as marketing tools. They put the author on-line. It's similar to a press tour without the travel, where people around the country can ask the author questions. The author participates either through his or her own computer at home or he or she can be on the phone with someone who has a computer. People on-line then type in their questions, and the author responds.

□ Will authors make money this way?

Not at this point. Today, it serves the purpose of promoting the author's work.

□ How will new media succeed in publishing?

We must learn how to create experiences that are compelling for the user, whether delivering information that's better than the printed version or providing entertainment that's different, and to a certain extent, better than books. If reading on a computer screen isn't better than reading from a book, the printed page will always win out. But if we can take characters, stories, and worlds from those books and do something different, something we can't do in a book, it could be a new experience that won't necessarily take away from the book. It may actually add to it. Many people go to a movie and read the book too. Or vice versa. They simply represent different ways to convey a story.

□ What advice would you give authors who want to get published and involved in the new media?

Get exposed to it. It's important for authors to see it. I always say that it would take me five minutes to solidly show someone some of the possibilities of what new media can deliver and an hour to discuss it with them and for them to only leave with a vague notion of what it is. At Bantam Doubleday Dell, we try to show our interested authors what has been done and encourage their thinking in this area.

It is important for authors to understand that each property must stand on its own. If someone writes a book with the ultimate goal of it becoming a multimedia title, they will more likely than not fail. A book must stand on its own and similarly, a multimedia title or new media title must stand on its own. One can't rely on the other to exist. If the book doesn't provide full entertainment value, it will have less of a chance to succeed. Similarly, if the multimedia title doesn't, it, too, will fail.

7

Who Are These People Called Editors?

What Do Editors Do? How Are Editors Trained to Do What They Do? Who Makes the Ultimate Decisions? How Much Clout Do Agents Have? And More

DAVID ROSENTHAL, EXECUTIVE EDITOR

DIVISION VICE PRESIDENT

Random House Adult Trade Books
Publisher Villard
New York

DAVID ROSENTHAL began his career as a reporter and editor with the *New York Post.* He entered the world of magazine publishing as executive editor of *New York Magazine* and managing editor of *Rolling Stone Magazine.* He served as editorial consultant to Random House, then joined the ranks and rose from editor to his present position as executive editor of Random House Adult Trade Books (since 1990). Rosenthal claims to be an editorial generalist, acquiring books of very literary fiction, serious nonfiction, and "extremely commercial properties." His books include *Vox* by Nicholson Baker, *Fatherland* by Robert Harris, and *Dance with the Devil* by Kirk Douglas.

Rosenthal's employer is the Random House imprint, Little Random, of Random House, Inc., which consists of Random House, Alfred A.

Knopf, Pantheon, Crown, Vintage, Ballantine Books, Fawcett Books, Fodors Travel Books, and, according to Rosenthal, "God knows what else." Founded in the 1930s, Random House is one of the largest publishing houses in the world.

□ **The editorial titles associate editor, acquiring editor, editor, senior editor, executive editor, editor in chief, associate publisher, and publisher—what do they mean?**
Titles mean nothing or they mean very different things to different houses. There are divisions among editors. There are editors at houses who work strictly on existing manuscripts that have been acquired by the house. "By the house" means books that have been acquired either by acquiring editors, who also edit their own books, or by publishers, who are primarily concerned with the business end of things, but also acquire properties.

□ **What are the primary jobs of an editor?**
The three primary jobs are acquire, repair, and publish manuscripts. In some houses, the editing role is divorced from the publishing role. Most editors at Random House operate as publishers per se, where the editors are intimately involved in every aspect of the production of the book—design, advertising, marketing, publicity, and so on.

It's the old cliché about the editor being the five-star general on his book. That's very much the way it works.

Job number one is using your taste to assess the commercial and literary merit of a work. The way that works is you read things. You decide whether this is a writer worth publishing, whether this book is worth publishing, whether this is a writer or talent worth developing.

The other job, which is critical, is to do whatever you can to assist that writer in creating the best book possible. Almost in a sense to be not so much the writer's master, but his or her slave—to be supportive, to be critical, to be essentially a very biased critic of someone's work. You want to do everything possible to enhance that work. Which sometimes means doing nothing.

□ **Are there cases in which editorial assistance is not needed?**
In the best of all possible cases, someone will turn in a manuscript that is sublime. Then you have the wonderful task of just signing a few pieces of paper to get the book into production.

□ **What about the writer who needs a great deal of editorial assistance?**
There are times when you need long and protracted editing sessions, discussions, talking cures, and things like that to help a book along.

□ What business decisions do editors make?

An editor in trade publishing decides to some extent how much of an advance a certain book merits, and how you can best not only recoup that advance for the house, but also make a profit on it so you can publish other books.

□ What qualifies editors to do all of these things?

The fact that someone empowers them. It's one of those jobs that involves living by your wits. It's like learning how to be a financial analyst or a lawyer or a doctor. It's a remarkable profession in so far as everybody is either overqualified or underqualified to do anything that involves more than buying an ice cream soda.

□ What determines editorial success once someone has empowered you?

A track record of having acquired x number of books successfully over a period of time, which have turned out to be successful books—books that are profitable or of great merit to the house and to the authors. If you buy twenty books a year and all of those books lose a fortune of money and all of them get lousy reviews, you're obviously not too good at this. If you buy twenty books a year and ten of them make money, a few of them break even, and the rest lose some money and they get some nice reviews and some lousy reviews, you're probably doing pretty well.

□ What are key ingredients of a successful editor?

You need to have taste, and that's in the eye of the beholder. And you need to have opinions. You have to back up your taste and your opinions with money, even if it is the company's money. The editor is ultimately responsible for how that money will be spent.

□ Must the editor's personal philosophy reflect that of the particular company?

I don't think companies have profiles, editorially. There are some houses that are more upscale than others. What any publisher is looking for in hiring an editor is somebody who is capable of attracting books to the house, either by his personality, by his taste, by his wit, by his perseverance, and then having those books be successful—at the very least, literarily successful, esthetically successful, if not always commercially so.

□ Are there means of acquiring books other than those initiated by agents?

I try to invent books. I know a lot of other editors do that too. The editor comes up with the idea for the book and goes to a celebrity or someone like that and tries to create the book. There may be an agent involved later, but the project may not be initiated with an agent.

□ Do agents have too much clout with editors?

Probably. The problem I see—and it's nothing I blame the agents for—is that editors and publishers have to some extent ceded their jobs to the agents. There's nothing in the entire world that prevents a publisher from doing the same thing. The agents are doing the publishers' jobs. The publishers should be reading the literary journals, should be going to the readings, should be lounging around. The agents are doing more of that than we are. That is a big part of the problem. There is no reason an agent should hear of a kid graduating from a writing program who is very talented before we do. The only reason that is the case is because we are not doing our jobs well enough.

□ How do you feel about the fact that an agent receives 15 percent of the book's royalties, while the editor, who works with the author throughout the development of the book, may get a promotion, but doesn't get those big bucks?

I have no resentment about that. That's the decision the author makes.

The agents perform, in most cases, a very valuable and difficult service. It's not just negotiating a deal. There are all sorts of other aspects that they do, such as being the salesperson for the overseas rights of the book, negotiating movie deals—all sorts of things that we generally have nothing to do with.

□ An agent sends in a manuscript and the editor likes it. What happens?

I can only speak of what happens here at Random House. The enthusiastic original reader would give the manuscript to one or two colleagues to look at for second opinions. If they are similarly favorable, the head of house would look at it, and, if it passes muster, would then talk to the editor and agree on a price to offer for the manuscript. You go back to the agent and say, "I would like to offer you x amount of money for this," and the agent is free to take it or leave it or what not. The negotiation usually involves the amount of money and what rights would be controlled by the publisher and what rights would be controlled by the agent and the author.

□ What range of advances does Random House offer?

From $0 and $1,000 to multimillions.

□ How is the advance determined?

The same way the other matters are determined. It's experience and a lot of rolling dice. You set an advance just a couple of ways. One is estimating how much money the book will earn in royalties and how much potential profit to the house, based on potential sales. When you look at a book, it's incumbent on you to say, "I think I can sell fifty thousand copies of this book, I think I can sell paperback rights for $100,000, I think this and this and this." You add up those numbers, and that should be your advance or thereabouts.

Sometimes in a competitive situation you may have to go higher. Another house may have done other calculations, which brought the numbers in higher. You have to take a gamble as to whether you think it's worth more. You may get into an auction situation.

□ Are there scientific methods in determining advances?

It is completely guesswork. There is nothing scientific about it.

We, like all other publishers, run computer models on any significant purchase. If we buy a book for a half-million dollars or we're about to make a half-million dollar advance, we put down some numbers as to what we expect a first printing will be, what we expect the retail price of the book will be, what we would anticipate foreign rights to go for, and so on. We run a computer model and see what we come up with as to how much we would make or lose on that advance or whether that advance would earn out for the author and for the house. You don't live and die by those, but it's a very useful tool. It seems scientific on the one hand, but then again you realize that the model is based completely on suppositions. I can put in a model that a book is going to sell 100,000 copies when, in fact, we're only going to print 15,000 copies. If you do that too often, you're going to be peddling newspapers on the corner.

□ Do advances ever have to be returned?

Never. The risk is the publisher's.

□ Is that written anywhere?

Yes. At least in our contract. I know of no legitimate trade publisher that requires an advance to be repaid. The only time that an advance is repaid is if the work is either not delivered to the publisher or the final manuscript that is turned in is deemed unsatisfactory by the publisher.

□ How often are advances returned because the manuscript is not delivered or the publisher finds it unsatisfactory?

Not too often. I think every editor goes into a deal with a high certainty that the author is going to deliver the book you expect. Sometimes they don't. Then you figure out what to do.

It's like being in a candy store: you broke it, you buy it.

□ What if there's a disagreement between the author and the editor on the direction of the book?

An editor will usually say, "If you don't want to do it that way, go talk to editors around town and sell it to another publisher." If the author finds another publisher, he will repay the original house and everybody's happy.

□ **How often do authors return advances and go with another house?**
I can't put a number on it, but it's certainly not a rare occurrence. Very often
an author turns in a book or there's an argument with an editor. Everybody
agrees it's in the mutual interest for the book to move to another house, assuming that another house wants the book. Everybody gets repaid and everybody's
fine.

□ **What if there's a disagreement and no other house wants the book?**
Then something's got to give. In which case I would say there are two pieces of
leverage. The editor has the leverage to say, "Either you do it my way or I'm
going to find the book unacceptable and then you're going to have to pay me
back my money and I'm not going to publish the book." Or the author says, "I'm
doing it my way and I can wait you out and I'm never going to deliver the book."
In which case, this can turn into thermonuclear war.

□ **Are there cases in which the publisher must sue the author for the
advance?**
Going after the author for the money is actually fairly rare, but it does happen.

□ **How should an author view his or her editor?**
In terms of dealing with an editor, I think you have to look at the editor as
somebody who is going to be your most important critic. There has to be an
extraordinary amount of trust between editor and author, which is fostered by a
great deal of respect and a great deal of affection for each other. I'm not saying
that you have to be really great friends to have a good editor-writer relationship,
but it helps. A lot of times the editor has to say to the writer, "This isn't
working." There's nothing worse, when someone has worked two years on a
manuscript and turns it in and has this wonderful look on his or her face and you
take it home and you read it over a few nights and you go and say, "I don't get it."
That's a very hard thing to say to somebody. It's painful, because you want the
book to work, too. You have a vested interest in it also. On the other hand,
when you tell authors, who tend to have fragile egos sometimes, that you really
love something that they've written and that you're going to do everything
possible to make it successful, you want them to believe you.

□ **What would you advise editors about dealing with writers?**
Editors should really be clear about what it is they want from you. With nonfiction, you want to make sure that the book you want to write is the book the
editor expects. And vice versa.

□ **You get to select your agent. But you can't usually pick your editor.**
You always can pick your editor because you don't have to do a book for a certain
person if you don't want to.

□ **That means you don't go with that company.**
That's right.

□ **Can you get a different editor and stay with the same publisher, or can the editor pawn the author off on another editor?**
There are instances where there are disagreements between editor and author and an author can ask, through the head of the house or through his or her agent, to get a different editor. Similarly, there are times when the editor can't stand the author anymore and says, "I can't work with you. You have to get another editor."

□ **Is that a black mark against the author?**
I don't think so. It depends on the circumstances. As in any business, there are some people who have a reputation for being difficult.

If your book is sent on submission to ten houses and only one house accepts the book, you link with the editor and you just can't stand him or her. You don't have to sell the book. Or you can sell the book and hope never to talk to the editor. That happens too. You turn it in. You can communicate by note.

□ **Must you be on the same wavelength with your editor because other-wise you might turn in a manuscript that he or she deems unacceptable?**
Right. Which is one thing you always want to avoid. It's a delicate chemistry. It usually works. In fact, it works 90 some odd percent of the time. It's rather amazing that it works as well as it does as often as it does. One would think it probably would work less well more often.

□ **Do you think editors are really necessary? Could authors do a job as well without editors?**
I think there's nothing as good as a good editor for any author. And I think any good author appreciates that. It can be very destructive to have a bad editor or one of no merit whatsoever. It depends on what the author requires. The editor is the sounding board, he's the Greek chorus, he's the voice of the public—all of these things. Sometimes it takes great wisdom in an editor to leave a book completely alone. If it ain't broke, don't fix it.

□ **Is the editor in charge of marketing and media decisions?**
Not in charge, per se. That's usually an associate publisher's job. At Random, the editors are very involved in that. It's sort of a collaborative agreement. The editors suggest the first printing of the book and usually suggest ways of marketing.

□ **Is it important that the author and editor see eye-to-eye in marketing the book?**
That's another thing a writer should have clearly in mind. Does the editor see selling this book the same way an author does?

I think it's very important for an author to have some expectations, but not unrealistic expectations. If you're writing a very serious novel about subject X, or you're writing a biography about an obscure nineteenth-century polo player, you cannot expect it, usually, to be a best-seller. And you cannot expect the house to spend $100,000 in marketing on it. Any editor who promises that he will is probably lying.

□ Do you have advice for authors in search of a editor?

First, find an agent. In order to get to an editor, you must have an agent. It's very hard to do it otherwise, particularly in fiction, unless it's somebody in a writing program. Usually, in a good writing program, one of the professors is connected to a house or an agent.

□ Why is publishing so difficult today—for the author in search of a good editor and publisher, and the editor in search of a good author?

I'll tell you one thing that I find somewhat troubling. Too many people think that writing and creating books is a relatively easy thing. For example, you're at a party, and somebody may be a dry cleaner or a plumber. They say, "I have such stories, I ought to write a book about it." You don't hear anybody say, "God, that was some incredible brain surgery; I should have been a brain surgeon." Or, "That was incredible, that guy climbed Mount Everest; I should have been a mountain climber."

For some reason, people seem to be imbued with a certain degree of chutzpah that I don't quite understand, and what that's led to, for better or worse—often for worse—is that all publishers are seeing more manuscripts than they can ever imagine, and it has slowed down the whole process of really looking at books. Somebody is going to read your manuscript or read part of it, certainly. But the amount of time it takes from the time it's submitted to the time it's read is getting longer because there's so much chaff.

There seems to be a presumption on many people's part that the only thing separating them from best-sellerdom is the attention of an editor. Usually that's not the case.

□ Are there many talented authors whose work is languishing because they are unable to get a publisher?

There are very few really good unpublished authors around, I think. Sad, but true. I think, for the most part, if there really is talent there, it will be found, it will be recognized.

8

The Developing Editor-Author Relationship

JACKIE FARBER, VICE PRESIDENT
AND FICTION EDITOR
Delacorte Press
Imprint of Dell Publishing
Bantam Doubleday Dell Publishing Group
New York

JACKIE FARBER majored in intellectual history in college. After graduation, she worked in advertising at Gimbels in New York. When she temporarily retired to marry and rear her family, she did freelance editing. She returned to the workforce at Bernard Geis Associates, a now-defunct publishing house that specialized in commercial best-sellers. According to Farber, she learned everything she knows at Geis, where she stayed about ten years and climbed the ranks from editor to senior editor. She then went to Delacorte for a few years, to Morrow for a few years, to Random House for a few more years, and then back to Delacorte; she has been vice president and fiction editor there since 1988. She specializes in women's novels and crime fiction. She has edited many best-sellers, including *Pronto* by Elmore Leonard, *Tunnel Vision* by Sara Paretsky, and *Whispers* and *Daybreak* by Belva Plain.

Delacorte Press is about thirty years old. It is in the Bantam Doubleday Dell group, one of three equal groups. Delacorte publishes thirty-six hardcover titles a year, all of which eventually go into paperback. "When we buy books, we buy them hard-soft," explains Farber. "The books that I buy go into Dell. My bent is commercial. Primarily we are thinking Delacorte and Dell."

□ **How does the editor-author relationship develop?**

It develops the same way any other relationship develops. You have to have an editor who is supportive and at the same time firm in keeping an author on the right track. I work personally with my editors. I'm a very hands-on editor, not only with authors' works, but with them as human beings. I know them and I like them, and they know me and like me. It's just the way I work.

□ **What if that doesn't happen?**

If that doesn't happen, a book could still be good, if the editor is good. But I like to think of my authors as friends. It's very possible that an author will not be happy with an editor or the editor won't be happy with the author if the relationship is strictly impersonal.

□ **Why are you trying to develop this connection with the author?**

When I sign up a book, I don't expect that I'm only signing up one book. We often sign up two books at one time. No editor wants to spend time developing and working very hard to establish somebody and have him or her say, "That didn't sell very well; we're going to go elsewhere."

□ **Do authors leave a publishing house when the first book doesn't sell very well?**

It happens often.

□ **Do you develop a relationship with authors just to counteract their leaving the company?**

That's not why you develop a relationship. Your authors really become your friends.

□ **Does the relationship between editor and author differ with nonfiction and fiction?**

It's very different with nonfiction. A nonfiction writer comes to you with an idea. It often depends on the subject. I have a writer whom I admire very much whose nonfiction book we're publishing, but I didn't like her next idea. She was determined to do it, so she's gone away. You nurture fiction writers in a different way that's professional. But I still like to establish a personal relationship.

□ **Who is responsible for the relationship, the editor or the author?**

That's hard to say. I keep in touch with my authors or I try to. I'm responsible for the relationship because that's how I think. But I always think I'm responsible for any relationship I get into. I suppose it works both ways. I think authors need somebody to listen to what they're saying and what they're worrying about and what their problems are. I think the editor's role is to be there and to be very supportive. This suggests an editor gets involved in authors' personal problems. That's not necessarily, or often, the case. The relationship is primarily professional and often personal to a degree that varies from author to author.

□ **Do you call your authors every so often if you don't hear from them?**
Yes. I often speak to my authors. I speak to Sara Paretsky at least once a week. I speak to Elmore Leonard at least once a week. I speak to Belva Plain once a week. I call Maeve Binchy, who lives in Ireland, every couple of weeks.

□ **If you don't call them, will they call you?**
They might. If they have a problem, they certainly would call me. If everything goes along swimmingly, why should the author call? Editors should call periodically to find out what's happening, unless it makes the author anxious.

If a book is due, it puts the author in an anxiety state, which you don't want. I don't like to call and say, "We're never going to be able to publish this in June if you don't get it to me by such and such a date." You have to use discretion, knowing when to call and when not to call.

□ **What about the author who doesn't have an editor like you, who is working along, never gets called, and feels a little put off?**
I think that happens a lot. If he's lucky enough to have an agent, he should complain to his agent. His agent should call the editor. If he isn't lucky enough to have an agent, I don't know what to say. He really is in an unfortunate spot. I can't imagine that an editor wouldn't stay in touch with an author. I've heard of such things, but most of the people I know don't behave that way.

□ **Do you ever have relationships that don't work out?**
Yes.

□ **What do you do?**
Generally, the author does something. It's usually the author who complains to the publisher that he admires the editor enormously, but "We just don't see eye-to-eye" or "Our personalities are different"or "We just can't get along."

□ **Will the publisher give the author a different editor at that same house?**
Invariably. Even if he's an author that you've signed up and nurtured. You'll discuss it. When a thing like that happens, it's generally mutual. It has happened twice in my rather long career.

□ **What does an editor do?**
First of all, an editor acquires a book.

I happen to be an old-fashioned, hands-on editor. When I sign up a book, I edit it. That's probably because I'm older. I think if I were very young and wanted to be the hotshot of all time, I would be very busy running around signing things up and letting somebody else edit it.

□ **How does the editorial process work once you have signed up the book?**

With fiction, generally, I wait until the manuscript comes in. I read it once straight through, trying not to make any marks on it, and I think about it. Then I read it again, taking very careful notes about what has happened in each chapter, reminding me of what's going on. I'm very scrupulous. Then I look over those notes. I'm constantly asking questions on my yellow legal pad. When I'm through with that, I write an editorial letter explaining to the author what I think is wrong with the book, how it can be changed, whether there's a character who isn't believable, whether there's not enough of a narrative drive—all of the things that make a book. When the revised manuscript comes in, I go through it carefully and generally it's okay. If it's not, we go through the whole process again. After that, it goes to the copy editor.

□ **What do you ask of the writer in your editorial letter?**

I ask for revisions. Some writers don't go off track at all. Everything is fine, except for some minor little things. Others—especially people who write commercial fiction and have no particular voice, but have a kind of electricity about telling a story—sometimes need help. I tell them, "This doesn't make sense, you can't have this character behave that way, you don't have enough action here, you have too much there." I can give very specific advice: "Why don't you add a third character? Why don't you make this person, whom you only talk about off-stage, a character in the book?"

□ **What do you want the author to do?**

Sit down and really write something. And not just explain. Not tell, but show. It's much easier to tell than to show. If you say, "Mary picked up the phone and called her father. Her father lives in Chicago. He was a butcher and he became a meat packer and eventually a robber baron," that's telling. You want to be able to see the father through that person's eyes. One of the ways you can judge a good writer is if he shows you something. You see it in action. You don't have to write adverbially. You don't have to say, "Mary looked at him cheerily." What you really want is for the reader to realize through what you've been writing that Mary is cheery.

□ **Are writers sometimes rigid when you give them advice?**

Yes. You have writers who won't make the changes you suggest. In the long run, it's the writer's book. It's not the editor's book. I think an author should be very careful to listen to an editor. On the other hand, I don't feel that if the editor suggests something that the author finds offensive, that he do it.

□ **Are books badly affected by the author's unwillingness to make the suggested changes?**

Often. That's one of the most infuriating things about reviews. You'll see a review that says, "This book needed a real editor." You have page after page after page of pleadings with an author to take this character out or to take two pages of distasteful prose out. And the author says, "No, I have to do it my way." We say, "Okay, in the last analysis, it's your book."

□ **What are the editor's most difficult tasks?**

An inferior book from an author who has a tried and true reputation. I'm talking about a commercial book, not literature. The editor offers many suggestions, but the author says, "I've done the best I can do."

Another difficult task is turning down a novel by somebody you love dearly. I recently had such an experience. We published a wonderful first novel. The second one came in and it wasn't working on any level. I had to judiciously turn it down in an encouraging way and say, "Shelve it, don't publish it, it's not going to help your career. But please don't take it anywhere else. That's not going to help your career either. Put it on a shelf. Sit down and think about the novel that you really want to write that has character, locale, and all of that."

□ **What endears one writer to you and not another?**

What endears you is if you admire the author's writing and the author's personality. Certainly not that he or she follows your instructions.

□ **Do you have pet peeves regarding the author's personality in this developing relationship?**

Yes. When I say to an author, "I think you need to do a lot of work," and I have spent a lot of time on the book, thinking for at least ten days about what needs to be done, with all the readings and writings and everything else, and then have the revisions returned in three days as a sentence here and a sentence there. That's not what an editor means by revisions.

Some pet peeves come primarily from a bad mix. Our personalities may not work together.

It's dismaying when you try hard to come up with a plot improvement and then have an author say, "That's ridiculous, that never would have happened and I'm not going to do it."

□ **Do authors turn you off in other ways?**

If you keep publishing one unsuccessful book after another by the same author, you get turned off after a while, even though you love that person and you love that person's books. You tell them to go elsewhere and, of course, that is the book that becomes a great big best-seller. It happens all the time. When only

7,500 copies of the first novel and 3,500 copies of the second novel are sold, we say, "Look, this isn't working out for us. You ought to go someplace else." The author goes to another publisher, and the next thing we know, he has a runaway best-seller. That's not because of the fit; it's because it wasn't working in this one publishing house. Wrong time? Wrong place? You never know with cases like this.

□ **Are there other reasons you've lost books that eventually became best-sellers?**
We've turned down books that became best-sellers because the author was desperate for more money. Let's say you sign up a true crime book that's ongoing. The author is covering a trial and you've signed it up for a hefty advance. Ultimately the advance is all paid out and the agent says, "We need more money. He can't finish this book unless you give us more money." The editor says, "Hey, wait a minute! I've been supporting this guy for three years. We've paid him all of this advance plus $50,000 more. We can't pay any more money. Take the book elsewhere and he can pay it back from the first proceeds." (This legal clause requires a writer to pay back the original publisher from the sale of the same work to a different publisher.) They can take it to another publisher, and the book can turn out to be a wonderful book and become a runaway best-seller. That has happened more than once. You do get back your money, but you don't get back the money you might have earned. By the same token, you just can't keep paying money out because you don't know what's going to happen.

□ **Do you have other words to the wise for authors?**
Authors should listen to editors. They should bounce ideas or suggestions off the editor.

9

The Editor-Agent Relationship
The Author-Agent Relationship

CAROLE DeSANTI, EXECUTIVE EDITOR

Dutton Signet
Division of Penguin USA
New York

CAROLE DeSANTI received a degree in English from Smith College in 1981, and subsequently attended the Radcliffe Publishing Procedures Course. In 1983 she moved to New York and took a job with Holt, Rinehart, and Winston, then a division of CBS. DeSanti shifted to editorial in 1984, moving to Dutton where she ultimately held the position of senior editor. She left to freelance in 1989, as the result of transitions in the company when it was acquired by Penguin USA. She returned in 1991, to publish a list that includes fiction and nonfiction, cookbooks, books on feminist and women's issues, and literary fiction. DeSanti has been executive editor at Dutton Signet since May 1993.

Penguin USA is the umbrella company of Dutton Signet and one of the largest publishing houses in the world. The company is divided into two major subsidiaries: Viking/Penguin (Viking publishes hardcover; Penguin publishes trade paperback) and Dutton Signet (Signet is the mass market line; Dutton is hardcover). Other imprints include Plume, a trade paperback line; Roc, a science fiction line; Topaz, a romance imprint; and Viking Studio, highly illustrated books.

Dutton Signet publishes about 360 books annually and receives more than ten times as many proposals.

□ **How do editors in large companies usually acquire books?**
In general from agents, but it's not unusual to negotiate directly with an author.

□ **What do agents do for editors?**
It varies widely. This is very much a business of people and relationships. Personalities and individual styles influence how agents do their jobs. Every agent has a different way of conducting business. Some agents feel that their job is to sell the book, get the book placed, and then they step aside. Other agents are a part of the process from beginning to end and assist the book in any number of ways.

□ **Do you and most editors court agents to get manuscripts?**
Yes, though the best relationships are those that develop over time.

□ **Do you have a few special agents that you work with?**
Yes. You develop relationships with people over time, over the course of a number of projects. I look for agents whose tastes are in synch with my tastes, people with whom I have a rapport or a resonance with in one way or another. That doesn't mean that I don't buy books from a wide variety of agents, because I do. But there is a small group of agents that I see regularly and buy books from pretty regularly.

□ **Should an author have an agent?**
Yes, I strongly advise it. The agent is an additional advocate, or member of the author's "team." An author is entering the publishing "game," so to speak, with a one-person team or maybe a two-person team. An author really needs as many people as possible on that team to help push the book, advocate for it, and generate interest in the project. It helps to have an insider who knows the business—who knows the rules of the business, the conventions of the business, and the language of the business, who can be such an advocate.

Also, there's a tremendous amount of flux and change in publishing and it can help to have someone who is on top of the changes to step in if the circumstance should arise.

Agents conduct themselves in different ways, depending on their strengths and interests. Some agents feel that their job is to place the book. When the next book comes along, they'll place that book. These agents are really wonderful at selling and don't want to get too involved in other parts of the process. They will usually step in if there's a problem, or when the marketing phase of the book comes along.

Others like to involve themselves in the whole process. It really is a matter of where their interests lie and what their client load is. If they have a lot of clients, they are going to be busy selling those clients' projects. If they have fewer clients, they sometimes play a larger role in an individual title.

It also depends on how long an author stays with an agent. Authors who develop long-term relationships with agents probably allow them to do different things over the course of their career, or over the course of several books.

□ Do authors sign with an agent for just one project?
Sometimes authors go to agents for a one-shot thing. They want the contract negotiated. They don't want to have to nag the publisher for royalty checks. Agents take care of that.

□ How can an author judge an agent?
The author must feel out the situation and ask questions up front. If you just want to sell your book and have the agent step out of it, that's something you should state up front. If the agent wants a more hands-on editorial relationship, are you comfortable with that? Or, if you really need an editor, is this agent comfortable in that role?

The author should feel some kind of connection with the person who represents him.

If you are a first-time author, I advise against using a first-time agent, especially if that person's publishing experience is sketchy or nonexistent. There are a lot of individuals, I think, claiming to be agents who have never, in fact, sold a project or negotiated a contract. First-time authors can make the mistake of too eagerly signing on with people who express interest in their work and claim to have contacts. I'm not saying it can *never* work out—books get sold in all kinds of strange ways! But, be a little wary. Try to gather as much information as possible to make an informed decision. Like any professional you are hiring, you want to have some good references, you want to know other people who have used this person. You might want to get the client list that the agent represents. Remember, you're the boss!

□ Are there pitfalls to authors in retaining an agent?
It's very hard to have the wrong agent. It can be disastrous to have an agent whom you can't communicate with, who you feel is not being a strong advocate on your behalf, who doesn't do for you what you want done. It's not helpful to have a very inexperienced agent, or one who has a bad reputation in the industry.

□ What if the agent you select doesn't work out?
Terminate the relationship, and look for other representation.

□ Who provides the agent-author contract?
Not all agents have contracts. Some of the finest agents use no written contract with their authors. It's a hand-shake agreement and what they are bound by is

the agency clause that appears in the contract between the author and the publisher. Lawyers often insist that the author have a contract that specifies clearly what the obligations are vis-à-vis the agent.

□ What is the agency clause in the author's contract?
The agency clause specifies the distribution of money, how they're to be paid, where they're to be paid, and specifies that the agent is authorized to collect the money on behalf of the author.

□ What are the qualifications of a good agent?
Experience in the industry, books sold, and books published successfully! Experience at an agency, or in some cases, people who have left publishing houses to become agents. But be careful in this area, as I said earlier.

□ What is the difference between the agent in a small versus a large agency?
Small agencies can be less stressful places to work if they have a solid client list supporting them. A less stressed agent is a better agent, in my view! On the other hand, a big company has an infrastructure of support that can come in handy—secretaries, assistants, and the like. Every agency, large or small, has its own culture and personality.

□ What is a standard agent commission today?
Ten to 15 percent.

□ Do you have pet peeves about agents?
I guess the *worst* situation for an editor is when she works with an author to develop a project, before there's a contract, and then an agent comes along and sells the book to another publishing house. *That* hurts! It's a real heartbreaker. But you'd be surprised at what these relationships survive!

□ Are agents ever harmful to the process?
Agents are generally not harmful to the process. In my opinion, the agents that are not helpful to the process are those that lack diplomatic skills. They'll be very adversarial during a negotiation, for example, but never assist the book after the check is cut.

□ How are agents helpful to the process?
By negotiating a solid, protective contract that takes into account the author's particular situation. By drafting collaboration agreements when authorship is joint. By maintaining good relations with the publisher. By helping generate interest in the book after it is published.

□ **Although agents officially represent the author, do you think they more likely serve the needs of the editor, since editors are their bread and butter?**

Everyone is everyone else's bread and butter in this business. Ultimately, the books themselves are *all* of our bread and butter. It's the author's royalties that are making the agents their money on an ongoing basis. Agents can go on and sell books to editors and collect their percentages, but over the years, if they don't have ongoing royalties from these projects, they're not going to stay in business. Traditionally, the agent's job is to take care of an author throughout the author's whole career, unless the author changes agents. We're all linked, economically, in this system. Certainly, the agent has to consider the publisher's concerns and represent the publisher's concerns to the author. And vice-versa. At the same time, the editor is representing the author's concerns to the publisher and the publisher's concerns to the agent.

□ **Is it fair that agents get a commission on a book's royalty throughout the life of the book, while the editor works hard to develop a book but receives his or her same old salary?**

I think it keeps editors honest. I don't believe that there should be a system where editors participate financially in the books. It's not the editor's book. It's not the agent's book either. If I were to argue for anything, it would be for a time limit on agents' percentages of the royalties. That would certainly be unpopular! But I don't think that editors should take a further cut of authors' shares.

□ **Do some editors feel they are not given enough credit for their hard work on a book?**

In general, I do think that editors feel beleaguered, overworked, and underappreciated a lot of the time. I don't know whether sharing in the royalty is going to solve that.

□ **What is the most important advice you can give authors?**

I think the key to a lot of this is to get yourself involved in the business of publishing. It really is its own world, with its own language and its own networks and its own systems. The more you know about it, the more you understand its internal dynamics, the better off you'll be. Don't rely only on your agent to understand the business for you. I think an involved, diplomatic, problem-solving, self-educating approach is needed among authors. Authors need to make a greater effort to understand the *whole* business of publishing—especially if they want to make a living as writers!

□ Do you have a philosophy of publishing?

My own mission is to make voices heard that have not yet been heard. To connect writers with readers, and to generate more than one definition of the word "profit."

□ What is your philosophy of writing and the writing process?

There are many reasons to write, other than getting an advance and getting published. The writing has to come first. There are too many authors out there worrying about their contracts before they immerse themselves in their writing. I think that publishing is suffering for that—books are suffering.

Readers are discriminating; readers know what they want, and they know what they like. They know if an author's novel is not as good as the previous one. They know if it's not fresh. A career always reflects that over the long haul.

I would really put in a plea for passion and originality in writing and in the creative process that leads to writing. That way, we'll have better books and happier readers who will come back for more.

10

The Editor-Agent Relationship
The Author-Agent Relationship

A Second Opinion

SUZANNE RAFER, SENIOR EDITOR
Workman Publishing Co.
New York

SUZANNE RAFER, Senior Editor at Workman Publishing, was an English major in college. After graduation, she moved to England. When Rafer returned to the United States, she began working for Workman Publishing. She has been an editor since 1974. Rafer's list is eclectic, but she is best known for books on childrearing and cookbooks.

Workman Publishing, founded in 1968, is a completely independent company. "We're a roll up your sleeves, dig in, and really work on your books in a big way kind of publisher," says Rafer. Workman publishes thirty, mostly nonfiction books a year, which Rafer describes as "usually unusual but solid frontlist and backlist books that are always interesting."

☐ **How do you acquire books?**
At this point, I usually do so through agents. Agents who have good relationships with editors and know what editors are interested in will be on the lookout. They'll steer a good author to him or her. Or an agent can find writers for book ideas that editors often get. There are agents that I work with over and over again. But we're always looking for new contacts. I try to meet or find out about as many agents as possible. I get tons of submissions from a lot of agents.

□ What makes a good agent?

Someone who can help an author develop or spot a good proposal and get it to the right editor. Someone who understands what the editorial and publishing process is like, who has an understanding of what it means to produce a book. Perhaps someone who has had experience editing books so that he or she understands what it means to turn in a manuscript that's viable, understands how long it will take to review a manuscript, understands the steps to getting a book out, and what they mean in terms of scheduling a book. A good agent keeps track of what his client is doing. If the author seems to be slowing down, the agent will figure out a way to keep to the schedule. With these understandings, he or she can relieve tensions that the author may have and also make it easier for the editorial process.

From my standpoint, somebody who has been an editor before makes the best agent. It's nice to get a well-conceived proposal. You want to feel that you're working with someone who cares about the author.

□ What does a good agent do for an author?

The agent should find the best publishing company, get the best possible deal, and make sure that everything goes smoothly for the author. An author wants someone who can speak for him if a situation becomes kind of sticky.

□ Should the agent keep involved in the development of the book as well as its acquisition?

Only in terms of keeping the author on schedule.

□ Is it fair that agents get commissions on book royalties for the life of the book and you don't?

That's how they make their money. That's their job. They're hired to find the right publisher for a book. Not every book sells a gazillion copies. The life of a book may be very short. The money may not be very much at all.

□ What standard fees do agents charge authors today?

About 15 percent. We pay the agent; the agent pays the author.

□ Will editors look at proposals submitted from agents before they look at proposals submitted from authors?

I do see that all manuscripts are reviewed, agented or not, but when I receive proposals from agents I work with, I'm more likely to look at them first. If I've got a stack of proposals to review, I'll look at something from an agent first because my time is very tight. It's not because nonagented writers haven't spent a lot of time preparing manuscripts. It's not because some of them may not be wonderfully publishable. You make the time for the people who may have something that will be right for your list. Because I deal with agents on a day-today basis, I don't want them to feel ignored. I wouldn't want to be ignored if I had a working relationship with somebody.

□ **Should all writers retain an agent?**
It's not a bad idea. You have to find someone you feel comfortable with. It's very hard. If you're a high-powered author who understands contracts, doesn't mind negotiating with the publisher, and can get a proposal to lots of people, maybe you don't need an agent. Nowadays, there are so many proposals out there, so many manuscripts that come in to people who don't have all that much time to read. It's good to have someone in there fighting for you.

□ **Are you annoyed when agents call you about proposals that you've had for a while?**
It can be annoying, but it's important that they do. You know agents are doing their job when they keep calling and nagging you if you haven't gotten back to them. At least you know the agent cares.

□ **Do you have advice for authors in search of an agent?**
It's tough. Authors have to do their homework. Agents are also very busy and they get a slew of manuscripts. Talk to friends who have agents and talk to their agents. There's a list of agents in the *Literary Market Place* (LMP). Be sure agents have expertise in the type of manuscript you're writing. If a publisher has already accepted your proposal, but you'd like someone to negotiate the deal, the editor may recommend a few agents who will probably do right by you. I've done that for some of my authors.

□ **Will you give more money to an agented author than to a nonagented author?**
I think the agent can make a difference. This is probably true at other houses more so than mine. We will offer what we offer, maybe with some change, agented or not agented.

□ **Will an author do better financially by retaining an agent for a second book?**
The value of the second book depends on how well the first book did. But everything is relative. Many things have to be taken into account. Some people will do a first book that is enormous in page count. And the next book is a ninety-six-page quick idea.

□ **How do you think agents feel about editors?**
I can't speak for agents, but I would hope they feel good about the editors they work with. I really enjoy working with my authors and I enjoy good projects. Of course, when I look at all the proposals on the floor that I haven't reviewed yet, I imagine there are agents out there wondering whether I really exist.

11

Queries, Proposals, Manuscripts
What Editors Want and Don't Want

Fiction and Nonfiction

REBECCA SALETAN, SENIOR EDITOR

Simon & Schuster Trade Division
New York

REBECCA SALETAN has been senior editor in the adult trade division of Simon and Schuster since November 1991. After graduating from college with a major in English, she climbed the publishing ladder from manuscript editor at Yale University Press to senior editor at Random House and ultimately to her present position as senior editor in the adult trade division at Simon & Schuster. One-third of Saletan's list is fiction, largely literary. Her nonfiction list includes issue-oriented books for women, pop psychology, self-help, true crime, popular science, journalism, and health. Saletan is editor to Elizabeth Marshall Thomas, Carrie Fisher, and Stephen McCauley, among others.

Simon & Schuster Adult Trade Division competes primarily with Random House, Viking Penguin, Bantam Doubleday, Dell, and smaller houses as well. "It depends on the nature of the book," says Saletan.

☐ **What do you and other fiction editors look for in a work of fiction?**
I'm looking for a voice, first and foremost. I'm looking for the writer's ability to create characters, scenes, and dialog. I'm looking for the ability to tell a story. I'm looking for the writer to sustain that over the course of the book. For me, character is more important than plot. The psychology has to be real and the

author's primary interest has to be character. Writers must be able to handle the mechanics of plot, but not be overly preoccupied with that to the expense of character. I also like things that are darkly funny and books that are ambitious. I don't like quiet little novels. With a first-time fiction writer who has never been published, we generally have to read the whole manuscript because there's no way of knowing whether he or she can carry it off.

□ What do you look for in the fiction writer's background?

It helps if the person has published before, even in small literary journals. Anything else that he or she can give me to go on, particularly with literary fiction, which is hard to publish and get attention. Frankly, my standards for literary fiction are extremely high. Unless I really fall in love with a book, I'm unlikely to take it. A book alone is a very difficult way to make your name. Previous experience—prior books or magazine publication—means there's some audience out there, however small.

□ What do you want in a nonfiction proposal?

It's a little different with nonfiction. The writing doesn't necessarily have to be as good. I've gotten excited about a proposal that was clunkily written because I could see that it was going to be important. I'm looking for an overview, a sense that the author is capable of dealing with structure. I want the confidence that the writer is capable of organizing the whole project and taking on a big thing like a book.

It's also important that the tone be good and reflected in the proposal, even though the proposal isn't the book itself. I want to know that the author can write in a way that an ordinary reader can read. Some writers submit a formal proposal. They're surprised when you react as if that's going to be the tone of the book itself. But that's what we have to go on. I also want a realistic assessment of whom the book is for.

I want a double-spaced, neatly prepared manuscript. We read a lot and it gets very hard on the eyes. A single-spaced manuscript makes me want to cry and run the other way.

People often think it's important to impress editors with fancy binders. The first thing I do is take the manuscript out so I can read it easily. Double spacing is the single most important thing. Fancy formatting is silly. Apart from that, there are not many rules.

□ Do nonfiction writers need credentials?

Yes. That's more important for nonfiction. Anything—fellowships, places they've taught. It depends on the kind of nonfiction. If you're writing a book on politics, previous experience in journalism or having been in somebody's administration would be helpful. In literary nonfiction or memoirs—books that are more like fiction—credentials are less important.

□ **Many writers get published in magazines without previous credentials.**
It's different with magazines. I might buy *The New Yorker* because the quality of the authors is generally good. I know what I'm getting. The same is not true for a publishing house. Readers don't go into a store and say, "I like the kind of books Simon & Schuster publishes. I'll buy this novel because I like the stuff they do." They need to be drawn to buy a specific book or author.

□ **Does a good proposal sent over the transom have a chance?**
I don't read everything that comes to me; my assistant screens. She's quick to point out something that's very good. One of the big misconceptions people have about editors is they think we sit here surrounded by masterpieces, trying to decide which of them to publish. We don't. We sit surrounded by masses of not-very-good writing and stuff that's just okay. I'm looking for something that absolutely captivates me.

□ **What is the major mistake that writers make?**
Overselling themselves instead of giving us a very good specific reason to publish that book. We're often looking for niches. We're looking to see that a book can compete in the marketplace—not that it's the greatest thing ever written. We must address market concerns.

□ **What should writers do to help editors with their proposal?**
Writers should realize that an editor is essentially an in-house advocate for a book. They should supply us with arguments, material, and the ammunition not only to acquire the book, but eventually to use while publishing it.

I'll take on something for pure love, particularly a novel. But the more ammunition that I have to do battle for it in-house, the better.

□ **What about typos?**
Some of my best writers are bad spellers. So I hesitate to even say that they should spell it correctly. I personally find it annoying to read something that's messily prepared or full of typos. Beyond that, just being clean and straightforward and not filled with all kinds of bells and whistles is very helpful.

□ **Is there a chance for unagented writers to get published?**
They should write to specific editors at houses that publish books similar to their proposed book.

□ **Do you have advice for authors in search of a publisher?**
Do your homework. Writers should understand that the problem for them is to get discovered. They should not oversell themselves, but write an intelligent,

direct, catchy cover letter and proposal for a nonfiction book. That would make me take a closer look.

If you're writing a child care book, for example, there are a zillion child care books out there. It would help your odds to say in the proposal, "There are five similar books on the market. This is what my book does that those don't and this is who it's for."

□ Do you make a distinction between fiction and nonfiction?

When I see good fiction, my hair stands up on end. I publish nonfiction because I think it is important or useful and I see an obvious market for it—even if it isn't elegantly written, even if it isn't going to be one of the things I want on my tombstone.

□ If a writer has talent and perseveres, will he or she get published?

That's too broad a claim for me to make. People in the business recognize quality. If somebody sends something of quality to me, my assistant is quick to call it to my attention. I'll look at the cover letter. I'll look at the first paragraph. If it's really exciting, I will pay attention to it.

12

Author-Editor Etiquette

JANET SILVER, SENIOR EDITOR

Houghton Mifflin Company
Boston

JANET SILVER has been at Houghton Mifflin, Boston, for ten years. She became editor in 1989. After earning undergraduate and master's degrees in English, she pursued a doctorate, at the same time working as managing editor of a quarterly magazine of literary theory published by the University of Chicago Press. She moved to Boston when her husband attended law school. According to Silver, writing a dissertation was not going to support them, so she did the only other thing she knew how to do: edit books. She freelanced, then accepted a position at Houghton Mifflin as a manuscript editor, rose to developmental editor, and began acquiring her own books when she was promoted to editor. She edits fiction and nonfiction, but literary fiction makes up the bulk of her list.

One hundred and sixty years old, Houghton Mifflin is a large textbook publisher with a very selective, midsize trade and reference division that is known particularly for its books on natural history and the environment as well as its distinguished list of literary works.

☐ **How do you acquire most of your books?**
Ninety percent are acquired through agents.

☐ **How do you acquire books that are unagented?**
I'm constantly writing letters to authors whose work I admire in magazines, and I attend writers' conferences. I also respond to query letters asking if I'd like to see a manuscript.

☐ Do fiction writers submit proposals?

Editors almost never buy fiction on the basis of a proposal. Writers almost always submit a complete manuscript.

☐ What should a good, professional, nonfiction proposal include and how should it be presented?

It should tell the editor what the subject is, why the author is the perfect person to write the book, why this book needs to be published, and what competing books are out there. It should demonstrate that the author is capable, not only of doing the job well, but of doing it in an outstanding way. The proposal should be well organized, very well written, and give just the right amount of information without overwhelming the editor with irrelevancies. A sample chapter is helpful.

☐ Are proposals that come through agents better than those from authors?

I can't say that all proposals that come from agents are well done. Some agents are much better than others in guiding the author through the whole process of putting together a proposal. But, for the most part, proposals that come from agents are better than ones that don't.

☐ What is the worst thing an author can do in a book proposal?

The worst thing is to fill the proposal with overblown claims and lots of exclamation points. I won't be convinced that a book is going to be a best-seller just because an author tells me so. That's a clear sign of an amateur. People who talk about the best-seller potential of their books are people who probably don't know what they're talking about. Proposals are a little bit like résumés. A lot of people try to impress an editor by being different and funny and just a little wacky. It usually doesn't work. Neither do misspellings, typos—all of those things make editors suspicious.

☐ Is it imperative that the author use letterhead stationery?

It's not a must, but it helps to look as professional as possible. A handwritten note on plain paper is not going to get you very far.

☐ What is imperative for the author submitting an unsolicited book proposal?

Credentials make a difference. Anything an author can do to bolster the argument that he or she has the credentials to write a book is going to help.

☐ Is it very bad when authors don't direct their proposal to a named editor?

"To whom it may concern"? It's not a good sign. A proposal that's not sent to a specific editor is not likely to get read. It suggests the author hasn't done the necessary homework to find out which editor at the house is best for that book.

□ **Do publishers read unsolicited proposals or manuscripts?**
A lot of houses don't. Sometimes there is a submissions editor who reads things that come over the transom. But many houses, including Houghton Mifflin, have dispensed with that position.

□ **How long should the author wait to contact an editor after the proposal has been submitted?**
If it was unsolicited, the author should give an editor at least a month to reply. Unsolicited proposals go to the bottom of the pile.

□ **Is it okay for authors to call the editor about submitted proposals?**
If you haven't heard anything, it's because the editor hasn't gotten to it. The more you bother someone, the less likely it is that you'll get a quick or sympathetic reading. If you do want to call, ask to speak to the editor's assistant to get an idea of when you can expect a reply.

Here is an example of the worst kind of author. I got a phone call from a doctor who had written a thriller. Before sending anything, he called my assistant and insisted on talking to me. He finally got me on the phone and talked to me for a half-hour. I could not get the man off the phone. He delivered the manuscript in person. As I could have predicted from talking to him on the phone, the book wasn't right for us. He wouldn't take no for an answer and continued to bother us with requests for information that we're not in the business of supplying.

□ **How do you feel about postcards enclosed with proposals requesting that the editor check off appropriate boxes indicating receipt of the proposal and response time—two weeks or four weeks or six weeks— and requesting that the editor promptly return the completed card to the author?**
I throw them in the trash.

□ **What do you think of the author who neglects to send a self-addressed, stamped envelope?**
The manuscript will probably get returned, but it is a courtesy to send a SASE. The author should always include one.

□ **What about multiple submissions from authors?**
That's up to the author, but he should let the editor know that he's also submitted the project to other houses.

□ **Don't agents frequently send multiple submissions?**
Agents frequently do multiple submissions. They know that there are four editors at different houses who would be good for a particular project, people who

might be interested. It can save time, too, although agents who make exclusive submissions expect a very prompt reply.

□ **Do you send personalized rejections?**
Serious writers deserve some personalized comments on their work. Some writers need guidance and I feel it's part of my responsibility to provide it. If I'm writing a rejection for a novel, I try to say what's wrong or what doesn't work for me. If I think there are some things that are right, I say that too. Form rejections are often sent to the same people who send those form reply cards.

□ **Do you ever reconsider a proposal you have rejected?**
When I send a rejection giving specific advice, I may receive a letter back saying, "Thank you for the response. I'm considering revising and would like you to look at it again." In that case, I'd say, send it in. I've bought several books—fiction and nonfiction—which came back to me revised.

□ **What endears you to one writer or one proposal?**
Good writing.

□ **Do you have pet peeves about authors?**
People who won't take no for an answer don't do themselves any favors.

□ **How do you offer a book contract to an author?**
You shake hands on the phone before anything else happens.

□ **What kind of money should a first-time author expect?**
Your expectations shouldn't be too high. You have to start your career somewhere. If it comes from the right house and the right editor, an offer for a first book should be considered very seriously, no matter what the money is.

□ **What do you advise authors who must negotiate their own contract?**
Reading and negotiating a contract does require some expertise and knowledge of the business. There are books on the subject, or you can ask advice from a friend who's been through it.

□ **What needs to be negotiated, other than advance and royalties?**
Various subsidiary rights—book clubs, translations, and so on—deadlines, payment schedules, a huge amount of fine print.

□ **After the contract is signed, who pays the bills when the editor takes the author to lunch?**
The editor. Once you are a member of the house, your editor is your parent and in charge of taking care of you. But try not to order the most expensive thing on the menu.

□ **Can the editor and author have a close working relationship when there is an agent involved?**
The relationship between the author and the editor can be more close when the author has an agent. An agent frees the author and the editor to stick strictly to editorial concerns. The editor-author relationship can get sticky when you're talking about money.

□ **How should the author-editor relationship develop?**
The author should try to establish a very open relationship with an editor. The author should try to listen as closely as possible to an editor's suggestions for revision and feel free to open the dialog at any point in the revision. An editor should encourage this dialog and keep the author posted at all stages of the publication process.

□ **How much communication between author and editor should there be?**
As much as the author and the editor feel there needs to be. If it's nonfiction, and the book hasn't been written, I expect the editor would propose seeing partials of the book as it develops. The editor would want to know what progress the author is making and what stumbling blocks the author is running into. It's incumbent on the author to send a good chunk of material before expecting too much from the editor. An author should expect a quick reply, not an immediate reply, a reply that demonstrates that the editor is either pleased or displeased with the progress and direction the book is taking, and useful and constructive suggestions for making it better. Then, it should be an ongoing process, back and forth. I don't think the author should feel reluctant to call the editor and say, "How are we doing here?" I think it's also up to the editor to maintain contact. I call my authors periodically to check in, to make sure that tie is not broken. It's hard to be an author, especially when you're publishing your first book. You feel insecure, you need hand holding. An editor should be there to hold your hand.

□ **Is this process ever negotiated into the contract?**
Frequently.

□ **How would it read in a contract?**
The first payment would be made on signing the contract, the second payment, for example, on delivery and acceptance of one hundred pages or two chapters, and final payment on delivery and acceptance of the full manuscript. But this varies from author to author.

□ **Should an author panic when he won't make the deadline?**
If the dialog has been ongoing, there won't be cause for panic.

□ **In most cases, can an author get an extension?**
Yes, if he or she has shown good progress along the way.

□ **In terms of etiquette, do you have advice for authors dealing with editors?**
Treat your editor just as professionally as you want your editor to treat you. As two professionals, you should be having a cooperative, constructive, ongoing relationship. If conflicts arise, you should deal with them directly, openly, and without hostility.

□ **Once the book is published and there is media coverage, how should the author behave? How can the author help, without being obnoxious?**
It depends on what the book is and who the author is—there's no general answer to that question. But everything the author does in connection with promoting the book should be cleared by the publisher.

□ **What is the difference between books that receive wide publicity and others that do not?**
There are books that are media-driven and there are books that are review-driven.

For books that are media-driven, the author is going to be very much an active participant—on talk shows, on radio, doing book signings. Often the book concerns an issue that has wide interest and the author is an authority on that issue. For a media-driven book, the author's "media-friendliness" counts. If the author is not good with media, he won't sell too many books. On the other hand, some books are so good, the media can make the author look good, too.

Review-driven books, which is what I primarily publish—especially literary fiction—depend on reviews for sales. The author should be available for readings, for signings, and for whatever other publicity the publisher wants to do to enhance review attention.

□ **What can authors do to publicize their books?**
Here's an extreme example of what an author can do for himself. One of our first novelists took the money that we had allotted for his limited tour and spent six months on the road in his station wagon, driving all over the country, visiting just about every single literary bookstore in the United States—just stopping in to sign stock, if it was available. He wrote to booksellers, saying, "I'm going to be in your town. Would you like me to come and say hello? Would you like me to do a reading?" He lined up his own radio interviews in conjunction with the readings that he was doing. He got a lot of press, all generated by his own efforts.

□ **Is this behavior acceptable to the publisher?**
Within limits, as long as it's completely approved by the publisher and the publisher's publicity department. The editor should be fully aware of what is going on and the publicity department should approve 100 percent. The author represents the company, as well as his or her own book.

□ **Do you have words to the wise for authors in search of a publisher?**
Do your homework. The most important thing is to find the best house for your book. Go to the bookstore and look at the shelf where your book would be shelved. Find out who publishes books like the one you want to write.

Look at the acknowledgments. Find out who the editors are for the books that you admire and are along the same lines as yours. Write a letter to that editor saying, "I very much admire the book by author X and I'm writing something that might appeal to you."

□ **Do you have words to the wise for authors in dealing with editors?**
If you're looking for an editor, write a query letter first.

Once you have an editor, remember that your editor is a busy person and yours isn't the only book that he or she is working on.

Require, too, that the editor pay attention when it's important.

It helps to have an agent involved because it keeps money matters and business matters to the side. An agent can be both matchmaker and advocate.

If you're not working with an agent, you need to be your own advocate. And you should expect your editor to be your in-house advocate.

13

What to Expect after Your Book Comes Out

Publicity, Book Promotions, Book Signings, Dealing with the Media, and More

ROBERT WEIL, SENIOR EDITOR

St. Martin's Press, Inc.
New York

ROBERT WEIL is senior editor in the trade division of St. Martin's Press. After graduating from college with a major in history and teaching with an eye toward the law, Robert Weil dabbled as an editorial assistant in 1978 at Times Books. After that, he never went to law school and never left publishing. Weil was promoted to assistant editor at Times Books, then went to *Omni* magazine in 1981, where he was features editor and creator of its book division. He moved to St. Martin's in 1988.

St. Martin's Press was founded in 1952 by Macmillan of London. The company consists of a trade division, which publishes 500 to 550 books annually, a mass market division, a science fiction imprint, and a college division, among others.

☐ **What can publishers do to promote a book?**
They can advertise. They can send authors on a tour. It depends on what the book is, who the author is, and what the audience is. More and more the trend is for authors not to expect this kind of huge money outlay. A tour of twelve cities can cost $20,000 and up, which is something most publishers can do on very few

titles. At many companies, the most expensive books will get the most promotional and advertising attention. It's a self-fulfilling prophecy. How well a book reads, particularly with fiction, is also a strong determinant.

□ What should first-time authors expect?

For a very good new novelist, a publisher can concentrate in a region, in one geographic area, and build the author in that area. This regional publicity will create word of mouth. Given the hugeness of this country and the fact that reviews are often impossible to get, doing something geographically may make perfect sense for a book.

□ Can the author influence the promotion budget? Do you listen to the author?

Absolutely. I always want an author's ideas. When the manuscript is completed and the editing is done, I always tell my authors, "Your job is only half done. Now the other half begins." Sometimes they're surprised by this comment. I consider it the author's job to help the publisher sell the book. The author can send out postcards to regional bookstores. The author can write for magazines and newspapers. We want an author who speaks, who is out in the public, who has some ability to sell a book. Any author who relies solely on the publisher to do it, unless he or she is incredibly famous, is deluding himself or herself, because it won't get done. The most successful author is the one who can cajole the publisher, through hard work himself, into doing a lot more than he ordinarily might have.

□ If the author receives major publicity, must he or she also do his own promotions?

My attitude is the writer should never take for granted what will be done. If you take for granted that everything will be done, you will have a very unhappy relationship with your publicist and with the company. The most successful author is the one who is filled with ideas, who can stir up excitement on the outside and create a spin, which goes into the publishing house.

□ What do you mean by a spin?

An author of a nonfiction self-help book, who gives a hundred speeches a year, is very attractive. That author is out there building an audience. We can help. We can get a reporter to where he is talking. We can get something controversial into a paper. We can build early interest. If we get a major article about a book just as it's about to be sold by our salesmen, bookstore owners across America will have seen it. When the sales rep comes calling, they'll say, "Oh, I just read about that in the paper. Sure I'll take two copies."

□ **Where does the editor fit in?**
It requires a very good editor to work with the author, encouraging the author in this way.

□ **Will the publisher financially support the author's attempts at publicity?**
Around book publication time.

□ **When does book promotion begin?**
Promoting a book starts at least a year before publication. By promoting I don't mean just getting reviews. The publisher's task is to take an author from one level and bring him to a much higher level by the end of the publication process of a book.

□ **Why do certain books seem to receive all kinds of major publicity at once? They get major print reviews, the authors are on all of the television talk shows. How is this publicity coordinated?**
A publicity department selects certain books and authors—often authors who are already quite well known or authors with a very successful first novel that sold thousands of copies. It will be very easy to get attention for the next book.

□ **What do publicists do?**
Publicists are critical to the success or failure of a book. They are responsible for creating the outside excitement about the book through the media—through television, through radio, through print, through marketing schemes that get people excited about the book. They know how to play a book. A literary novel gets publicized in an entirely different way than a nonfiction joke book. Publicists and marketing people determine the best way of doing publicity and marketing for that book.

□ **How do you feel about publicity blitzes for big-time authors?**
Everyone likes a winner. That's one of the major problems with American publishing. People jump on the bandwagon too easily.

□ **What about publicity for a first-time author with a very compelling book?**
That's what we call a "make" author—someone you have to make into something, someone who has not appeared previously in *People Magazine*. I prefer that kind of author because it's more of a challenge. It shows that you can really publish. The author has to have some fire within himself as well.

□ **What of the author with a controversial, thus promotable book, who isn't telegenic?**
I wouldn't care if the author couldn't go on television. You can do wonderful things in print with a controversial book. For a nonfiction book of a very

controversial nature, I would strongly look for someone with the qualifications to write that book.

If someone with a background in Chinese literature writes the most compelling book about legal decisions regarding abortion, I will have trouble because that is not the right person to deal with one of the burning issues of the day.

□ What if an author refuses to appear on television?
If you pick someone who says, "I won't appear on television," you should do the book in a different way. I personally don't like to go on television. Some people hate it.

□ Do publishers prepare authors for television appearances? Are there tricks?
If you have people who are suddenly doing major shows and appearances, who have never appeared before, trained publicists teach them how to appear properly, speak properly, and guide them in what to say.

□ What about bookstore signings? Who sets them up? Who pays for them?
The publicists and marketing people. If we want to develop a novelist in a certain region and do a four-state author signing, publicity will call ten or twenty accounts and say, "We want to send you this galley. We think this is very special. Will you consider this for a book signing?"

I've also had authors set up their own signings. They have relationships with bookstores. That's great. They must confer with their publicists.

To do a book signing, the publisher must put up co-op money, which the bookstore uses to advertise the signing. You can easily spend $8,000 to $10,000 in co-op money on a whole promotion tour of signings. It can be expensive because many bookstores often won't do it without the money.

□ Are book signings financially successful?
It depends on the author and the region of the country.

□ Are you saying that some regions of the country are more supportive of their authors? Can you give me an example?
Oklahoma is incredibly loyal to its writers. If a publisher gets a first novel or a new work of nonfiction by someone from Oklahoma, you'll get a good number of people to signings out there because it's a big deal. If we set a first-time author out on Fifth Avenue in New York and his or her friends don't show up, the signing will be a failure. The author won't get a reception in New York unless the book has some critical following in the press.

Authors can be very embarrassed if book signings don't work. We have to warn authors. You can get three people at a signing. Writers have to be tough and just go on to the next.

□ Do authors ever hire their own publicists and set up their own tours?
It happens. Often it's not coordinated that well with availability of books in the bookstore. You can have some disappointing results.

□ What is the goal of publicity for a book?
To build up word of mouth on a book, to create demand for what you have written, to get people talking about it and passing it to each other and saying, "This moved me, this brought me to tears." The goal is to find the demand. It can be anything—from the most literary of works to the most commercial diet book. The author has to ask, "Where is my audience? How can I get to it most effectively?"

□ Do you have other advice to authors in terms of book promotion?
You have to love what you're doing. You have to love people. People who buy books will be with you for life. They're sacred to you.

The most effective authors are the ones who will talk to everyone. The concern has to be genuine. If that concern is there, the readers will know it and they will be very loyal. The next book won't be as difficult because that audience is beginning to build.

It's the same with your relations with a bookstore. The owner of that bookstore is your advocate. If you have a relationship with him and you were successful with your previous signing—even if wasn't successful, yet something clicked—that bookstore owner is going to remember you and will want you again. The trick is to build up a following.

It's hard work. It takes modesty. It takes a lot of love. It takes talent. You can't do it without the talent. It all has to be there. When that rare combination exists, you will endure.

14

Movie Tie-In Books

ESTHER MARGOLIS, PRESIDENT AND PUBLISHER
Newmarket Press
New York

ESTHER MARGOLIS, President and Publisher of Newmarket Press, was an education major in college and earned a master's degree in English. Her first job, in 1961, was secretarial, in the promotions division at Dell Publishing. After one year she went to Bantam Books as a promotions assistant and became its first publicity director in 1965. She stayed at Bantam for seventeen years. Margolis eventually rose to senior vice president, overseeing all of the marketing departments; she instituted many innovations, including the first author tour, a model for the industry. By the early 1970s author tours became popular and are now a major component of book marketing. Margolis left Bantam in 1980 to start Newmarket, a publishing and communications company that includes Newmarket Press, the publishing imprint.

Newmarket Press publishes about fifteen mostly nonfiction books a year in the areas of self-help, child care, parenting, and popular reference and film, including the companion books to *The Age of Innocence*, Bram Stroker's *Dracula*, and *Dances with Wolves*. "We're a small, independent press," says Margolis, "but we're mainstream. Some of our books have sold over three hundred thousand copies." Margolis also consults on publishing, marketing, and novelizations for such film studios as Columbia, TriStar, and Universal Pictures.

☐ **What are movie tie-in books?**
If you take the words "movie tie-in" away and look at these books as companions to feature films or television presentations or other events, you get a better sense

of what they are. They're not unlike art books published in conjunction with museum exhibits or news related books published on top of today's headlines. They are all what I call cross-media or event books and are intended for a book buyer with a whetted appetite for more story, more knowledge, more lasting images.

□ Are movie tie-in books ever risky for the publisher?

Movie tie-in books are considered risky because they are marketed against an event over which the publisher has no control. The studio has the control. If the movie is destined not to work, the studio could pull it out of national distribution in a week's time.

□ Do movie studios have a financial connection to novelizations?

Yes. The rules of novelizations as a form are dictated by the Writer's Guild of America. The studio and, in most instances, the screenwriter participate in revenues generated by novelization.

□ What are the major types of movie tie-in books?

Reissuing an old book is one type, like *Schindler's List*. You get another shot at promoting it. When a major studio releases a movie, the publisher of the original work has the opportunity to ride with what will probably be at least a $20 million advertising campaign, not to mention the word of mouth that can be generated after people see the movie. If a movie is marketed as a major film, somebody other than the publisher is spending a lot of money to make that title work.

The originals are novelizations—novels based on a screenplay. Novelizations have become very popular in the last fifteen years; "making of" books about the movie; and nonfiction books about the research and background. You must have the book out in time for the film's release. To do that, you start working on it six to twelve months before the movie's release. The timetable is very tight. The writer assigned to a project usually has no more than six or eight weeks to complete it. For example, there's a new western in production. We were given the project three weeks ago to set up a novelization. The movie is coming out in five months. I have to hire a writer, deliver a manuscript, and have all of the artwork approved within that time. These things happen very fast. Once movies are "green lighted," they are made on a much faster schedule than books are. Successful ones include *Rain Man, Karate Kid, Fisher King,* and *My Girl.*

In fact, *The Karate Kid* was written as a novelization by a young woman who writes award-winning books for young people. The New York Public Library cited it as one of the top twenty-five books taken out by young adults. Many people today don't realize that *The Karate Kid* book was a screenplay first, then a novel. A novelization can last beyond the life of the movie. The better the novel and the more suited to a particular genre, the better chance it has of being successful.

□ Who writes novelizations and how much are they paid?

A novelization is usually assigned as a separate commissioned work to a writer on a work-for-hire basis. He may negotiate to have some royalty points. It depends on what he brings to the table.

Writers are paid between $7,500 and $10,000. Some of the more experienced writers get paid $10,000 to $12,000. But that's it. Royalties are about 1 percent.

□ Who hires writers to do movie tie-in books?

Movie tie-in editors at mass market publishing houses, or someone like myself who is a packager for the studios or the producers, hire writers.

□ How do writers learn this skill?

Writers need to have somebody take them through it. I have introduced the form to a few writers. I wanted to help these writers. I thought they could handle it.

□ Do you have a cadre of writers you can call on to write novelizations?

All publishers do.

□ How could a writer become a part of your cadre of writers?

They should have solid fiction writing experience and a track record in terms of delivery. Most writers are represented by agents.

□ How do novelizations differ from an author's other work in terms of ownership?

First, unlike the author's normal writing, in which he is possessor of the copyright, this is not his work. The studio holds the copyright. Second, the writer is doing something with his skill and his experience—taking a story in one form and adapting it to a novel form without having to create a story or characters.

□ Are movie tie-in books a good market for writers?

Only for a small number. There's not a lot of this work available.

□ Do big-name authors write novelizations?

Yes. In the 1960s, there was a very clever movie called *Fantastic Voyage*, starring Raquel Welch, which took a tour of the human body. The movie tie-in editor at Bantam asked Isaac Asimov to do the novelization. He thought it was a kick. His novelization of *Fantastic Voyage* is still in print today.

□ **What would you advise authors who would like to write movie tie-in books?**

This is a very limited market. Identify the movie tie-in editors and get them to consider adding you to their stable of writers.

Read a whole bunch of novelizations. Go to a bookstore or a library and read a few scripts.

□ **What is the chance that an inexperienced writer will get hired?**

It's a one in a zillion shot. But, as in life, anything could happen.

15

Book Packagers: The Editor's Viewpoint

SARAH DUNN, COPY EDITOR

Rodale Press, Inc.
Emmaus, Pennsylvania

SARAH DUNN has been a copy editor at Rodale Press since 1991. She was editor at Yankee Books, an imprint of Rodale Press, from 1992 to 1993. After graduating from college with a degree in psychology, she ran a research lab and worked in construction management before accepting her present position. When Dunn was at Yankee Books, she hired book packagers. She presently works with them.

□ **What is a book packager?**
A book packager is someone who takes on many publishing tasks that are normally done in-house—editing manuscripts, copy editing, design, layout, and indexing. I've worked with packagers who presented me with a proposal and had the book written as well as copy edited—they handled the entire project.

A current term is book producer. If they don't package the book themselves, they contract for it. They can deliver a finished package, even if they do none of the hands-on work themselves.

□ **Why do publishers need book packagers?**
Overhead costs. You don't have to beef up your staff to publish that wonderful book. It's much more expensive to add an in-house person than to hire someone outside as a freelancer. You oversee the project and make sure it meets your standards and needs. A good packager will do almost all the work for you.

□ How do publishers find book packagers?

I picked several out of the *Literary Market Place,* based on how they described themselves and their geographical location. There are so many packagers that it's very easy to find competent ones who can meet your needs. I would hire a packager who had experience and had published in the specific area that I was looking for.

□ How does one become a book packager?

You need to have access to or know people who have computers and can do layout and design. If I wanted to package a book for a publisher, I would find a designer, a copy editor, an indexer, an editor who specializes in the topic of the book, an illustrator (if there is artwork), and a photographer (if there are photographs). A book packager puts together the pieces and manages the project. Packagers are people who have left publishing houses, are out on their own, and have contacts from before.

□ How are packagers paid?

If they are simply taking the manuscript and making a book out of it, they are usually paid a one-time fee—work for hire. If they are also accumulating the information and writing the book, they may have a share of the royalties as well.

□ Do large as well as smaller publishers use book packagers?

Large publishers use them quite extensively.

□ Is the contract between the publisher and packager similar to that between a publisher and author?

If the packager's writing the book, the contract is very much like an author contract, but it also includes contracting for the design, copy editing, and indexing—it's a little more extensive.

□ How are book packagers paid?

They usually get paid a flat fee for packaging the book. They may also get an advance against royalties. In some cases, the packager can negotiate a copublishing deal and get a share of the publishing profits as well.

□ How does the book packager-editor relationship work?

The editor works with a packager the way he or she would work with an author, a designer, and a copy editor. The editor usually works with a point person who disseminates information to the rest of the packaging team. Also, the designer or art director of the publishing house may interact with the packager's designer.

□ Would you advise authors to have contacts with book packagers and publishers?

It's worthwhile for the author to have contacts with both packagers and publishers. If I have a book that I want packaged, I may suggest an author to the packager. Or I may call the packager and say, "Here's a book that I'd like you to do. Do you have an author in mind?"

It's good for writers to know packagers because projects may come up that they might get involved in. The disadvantage for authors is that they usually get lower royalties. Also, they have two editors—the packager's and the publisher's.

□ **Do authors work for hire, or do they receive a share of the profits?**
It varies from book to book and contract to contract.

□ **Do you have advice for authors who want to go this route?**
Contact packagers. Let them know your specialties. Let them know what you've done before. Send samples. Work with packagers to develop proposals that cater to your specialty. The specialty market is where it's going.

16

Book Packagers:
What They Do for Authors
and Editors

SANDRA J. TAYLOR

FORMER EDITOR WHO IS A BOOK PACKAGER

Sandra J. Taylor Literary Enterprises
Hancock, New Hampshire

SANDRA TAYLOR majored in English, but had no specific plans after college. She got into publishing accidentally when she moved to New Hampshire in 1972 and applied for a job at *Yankee* magazine. After six months as a secretary, she became an assistant editor. Taylor spent eight years with *Yankee* magazine, then moved to the book division there for nine more years, where she rose from editor to senior acquisitions editor.

In 1989 Taylor moved to Vermont. She was hired as editorial director of Camden House Publishing, a Canadian owned company that was starting a book division in the United States. Through her work with *Yankee,* Taylor had set up a network with agents in New York, the District of Columbia, and other parts of the country, and had good contacts with writers. At Camden House, the editorial staff was so small that Taylor began assigning much of the editorial work to freelance editors, copy editors, proofreaders, and the like. She would oversee the production of each project, while acquiring all of the books. "There seems to be a natural progression from an editor of books and magazines to a book packager," says Taylor. "I have had the opportunity to see publishing from the very beginning stages through the finished product."

In 1992 Taylor moved back to New Hampshire, where she started her book packaging company. She packages between five and ten books a year.

□ **How many book packagers are there in this country?**
There are more than one hundred listed in the *Literary Market Place.*

□ **How many published books have been "packaged"?**
About one of every six books in 1990 was a packaged book. It's becoming an accepted way of dealing with books.

□ **Why do you think book packaging is expanding?**
Book packaging has been around about twenty years and continues to expand. It allows publishers to bring out more books each season. It also enables a new imprint or new publishers to become established more quickly.

It's a time saver. Editorial staffs are so overworked. I know from my experience as a book editor, there is just so much time in the day. You've got manuscripts coming in, you've got to read and review and accept or reject, bring them before an editorial or marketing board, plus edit the material that's been accepted. Book packagers not only can relieve the workload, but also can provide quality control and hands-on attention to each book project.

□ **How far can book packagers go in the publishing process?**
A book packager can do anything from simply acquiring a manuscript for a publisher to delivering finished books. The publisher and packager negotiate what is to be done. Whatever book packagers do relieves the publisher of that much work and enables them to increase the number of books they can produce.

□ **Do small as well as large publishers use packagers?**
Some small publishers are reluctant to use book packagers because they are afraid of losing control of a project; they are used to having hands-on control all along. But book packagers can help publishers, both large and small, whether they are trying to increase the number of books they are bringing out or take the workload off the in-house staff.

□ **How can you put together a book more efficiently than a publisher?**
I hire excellent freelancers who are price competitive and have the time to devote to a single project. Instead of trying to juggle a half-dozen books at the same time, a freelance editor can concentrate specifically on this project and turn it around in a shorter period of time. Saving time also cuts costs. We have the ability to focus on each stage of production. As an in-house editor or copy editor, you never have just one project to focus on. You have to divide your time among a number of books.

□ **Please give me an example of how you keep the publisher involved at various stages of a book's production.**

I'm compiling a cookbook that I'll deliver on a camera-ready disk. I'm handling the whole project. The publisher sees the book at various stages. Right now they're looking at all the recipes that I'm considering, giving their approval, disapproval, or comments. I will show them the manuscript in rough form to review and make comments on. When the manuscript is final—edited, copy edited, on disk, and so forth—I will send it for one more review. They will look at the art concepts and give approval for the illustrations at various stages. There are no surprises for either publisher or packager. When one continues to work over time with the same company, and they become familiar with your style and taste, trust is set up and there may not be the need for involvement in so many stages. But this varies from publisher to publisher.

□ **Do book packagers have specialized areas?**

I tend to look for and propose books that I'm familiar with and can judge the quality of. I'm more effective sticking with books that I'm familiar with. Other packagers, however, have the staff and expertise to cover a broad range of categories.

□ **How can writers connect with packagers?**

The easiest first step is to refer to the *LMP* or contact the American Book Producers Association. As a book packager, I'm always interested in finding writers who have experience in the categories I'm looking for—nature, natural history, environment, country lifestyles, cooking, gardening. I clip articles that I've read in a magazine or newspaper with the intention of getting in touch with the writers to see about ideas they might have or projects they might be interested in doing for me.

□ **Is it easier for a writer to get published with a packager than with a publisher?**

In a way, it might be, especially for an unpublished writer. There are a lot of larger publishing houses that don't look at material from unagented writers. I think there would be less resistance in going through a book packager than a publisher.

□ **Should writers submit a book proposal to a book packager as they would to a publisher?**

If they have a specific idea that they want to propose.

□ **How do you pay writers?**

When I use a writer, it is a work for hire situation. I pay a flat fee for the project. But other arrangements can be made as well.

□ Why would an author accept a flat fee?

When an author is paid a flat fee, she's often getting at least as much, and in many instances more, than if she's paid an advance. Books often don't earn out the advance and these days publishers seem to be cutting back on the amount of their advances.

Another advantage is that you're guaranteed that money (assuming, of course, that the manuscript meets the standards and requirements of the packager). Some publishing houses are quick to remainder books and you never get to earn royalties.

□ Do authors ever earn royalties when working with a book packager, and what are the royalties?

Sometimes, but the amount varies tremendously, depending on the arrangement set up between the author and packager.

□ If an author comes to you with a book proposal that is accepted by a publisher, who offers the contract to whom?

It can be done a number of ways.

If a writer comes to me with an idea to propose to a publisher, I could consider myself an agent, negotiate the contract for the writer, and take a commission; the publisher then takes care of the production of the book.

Or I could act as the agent/packager. I would place the book with the publisher and produce the work. The budget and cost of the book would be reworked, based on the author arrangement. As a packager I would proceed with the book as with any other project. The author is already part of it. I would farm out the editing, design, and art.

Sometimes larger packagers will have a contract with the author and another contract with the publisher. They will pay the author a portion of the advance and royalties from their pocket.

□ Do you have advice for authors in dealing with book packagers?

Have a good feeling about the packager you're dealing with. Both sides want to be clear on what they are getting or giving. A first-time writer might need to submit a completed manuscript before the publisher or packager accepts it. Over time, trust develops.

Attend writers' conferences, seminars, and workshops.

Network. Don't hesitate to ask others about their connection to a publisher or packager.

17

The Small Press

ROLLIN RIGGS, EDITOR AND PRESIDENT
Mustang Publishing Co., Inc.
Memphis, Tennessee

ROLLIN RIGGS founded Mustang Publishing in 1983. He serves as editor and president, and is Mustang's one and only full-time employee. "Since Mustang is a one-man show," says Riggs, "I do everything—from acquiring and editing manuscripts to answering the phone to balancing the checkbook."

According to Riggs, Mustang is a small press with annual net sales between $250,000 and $500,000; it publishes only general nonfiction aimed at eighteen-to-forty-year-old readers, including how-to, travel, humor, and more. Mustang publishes six to ten books a year and receives approximately one thousand queries and proposals annually.

☐ **How do you usually acquire books?**
Most books come in the mail as blind proposals. Occasionally an agent will submit a book. Sometimes I come up with an idea for a book and seek out an author. Frequently, an author who has submitted a blind proposal through the mail, which I accepted and published, will come up with another idea for a book. So I'll get two or three books from one author.

☐ **How often do you work with agents?**
Less than 10 percent of the time. There's really no tangible benefit for an author who's not a professional writer and who's looking to get his first or second book published to have an agent. In that case an agent is just going to take 10 percent of a very small amount of money to begin with. I do think agents are valuable when the money gets bigger and more complicated.

□ **What kind of advances and royalties do you offer?**

It depends on the project. Generally, we offer an advance between $500 and $1,000. Sometimes we offer no advance; sometimes if the book requires a great deal of traveling, a little more. Our royalties range between 6 percent and 9 percent of the retail price.

□ **Why is it advantageous for an author to work with a very small publisher?**

First of all, when you call up, you know you're going to talk to the boss. There's only me! I have freelancers do a great variety of things, but I answer the phone.

It's a much more personal, hands-on approach to publishing than you find at a large New York publisher.

□ **Are the chances of making money lower with a small publisher than with a larger publisher?**

No. I think they're the same. They're low throughout. But I believe that your chances of having a happier publishing process are much greater with a smaller company than with a larger company. The odds of making any real money from a book are very low for an author—for a publisher, too, but especially for an author. You do it for personal satisfaction, for the challenge, for the creative process. If you don't get happiness from those three areas, and you don't make any money, you've wasted a lot of time creating your book.

□ **Why do you think an author will have a better experience with a smaller publisher?**

Because the author will get a more personal, hands-on approach to the editing and the marketing and the design of the book. The author has a lot more influence in the final product and has a lot more say in how that book is going to look on the shelf with a small publisher than with a large publisher.

□ **How does book distribution work with a very small publisher?**

That's the sticky part of working with a small publisher. The larger publishers have vast, powerful distribution networks set up. Small publishers have a harder time convincing stores to carry their books, and they have a harder time con-vincing consumers to buy the books off the shelf, because the small presses don't have the marketing and advertising budgets that large publishers have.

Most of the good small publishers are allied with a distribution group where thirty or forty small to midsize publishing companies combine efforts through one distributor. This distributor issues its own catalogs, has its own sales reps around the country, and has its own marketing program. So publishers can do things as a group that they couldn't do individually.

□ Do these distributors break into the national markets for you?

If they're any good they do. That's why you have a distributor. For example, a major chain store like Walden Books won't talk to Bill's Publishing Company. He comes to them with three books. He's not worth their time. It costs too much to set him up in their system and to deal with his books. They'd never make any money. But, if the distributor shows up representing forty or fifty small to midsize publishers, then, clearly, it's worth the chain's time to deal with him, and the publisher has a much better chance of getting books into the major stores.

□ Who pays this distributor?

The publisher usually pays a percentage of net sales for the year for that service. Most publishers who are serious about publishing—if it's not just a hobby for them—are happy to pay, because the arrangement frees up limited capital for other things—editing and design and other marketing programs—rather than paying to staff a warehouse and paying to hire someone to do all the invoicing and collections and paying someone to log returned books. All those real down-and-dirty issues involved getting books from point A to point B cost a lot of money, and I'd rather pay a distributor to take care of it.

□ How does the small publisher advertise and market books?

For a small publisher, unfortunately—and this is the big difference between small and big—a small publisher has to spend a lot of his advertising and marketing money just convincing the stores to carry the book. There's not a lot left over for consumer advertising and marketing. Usually small presses rely on reviews and feature stories in the press to lure consumers into the stores to get the book. Often they rely heavily on the author, especially the author's ideas. A lot of times the authors belong to trade associations and clubs, and they can market the book very effectively through those areas.

I can only speak for myself. I'm sure every small publisher does it differently. I tend to be very liberal in sending out review copies. It's a very inexpensive way to promote the book. At the very least, if a newspaper writer or editor doesn't review the book, he or she is going to know about it and maybe a month from now at a cocktail party someone mentions the topic and he says, "I got a review copy of a book about that a month ago." Now you've got word of mouth on it.

My personal experience has been that advertising to consumers, in general, doesn't work because you just don't have the volume of sales to justify the expense. Most advertisers are selling cigarettes or soap and they're selling millions of units based on their advertising. With books, you're happy if you sell a few thousand units.

□ Do you get the media to cover your authors?

Yes. We've been very successful in getting a lot of media coverage for our authors. That's been one thing we've probably done better than most other small publishers. We've had authors on the "Today Show," on National Public Radio, in the *New York Times* and the *Washington Post,* and *Playboy* magazine, and you name it—we've had reviews everywhere.

□ What are some of your well-known books?

Our best-selling book by far has been *The Complete Book of Beer Drinking Games,* with over five hundred thousand copies sold. *Medical School Admissions: The Insider's Guide* is the top selling guide to getting into med school. Probably in terms of media coverage and vast acceptance of a concept, the book I'm most proud of is *Essays That Worked* by Boykin Curry and Brian Kasbar. These sophomore Yale students approached me in 1986 with an idea to do a book on application essays for Ivy League schools. We discussed it. "Why limit it to Ivy League schools?" I asked. "High school students all over the country apply to state schools and other private schools that require application essays, and they're anxious about it. Why not get a wide variety of schools?"

They agreed to interview admissions officers, collect fifty of the best essays, and write a book that would show, by example, how great the college application essay can be and how important it can be to the application.

The book came out in the fall of 1986 and really took off. We worked hard to promote it to education writers around the country, especially newspapers. We got a feature story in the *New York Times* about the book. What really helped was the quality of the essays in the book. They were interesting and unusual. Teachers started buying it, and parents were buying it for their high school students. It was a hit.

The authors were interviewed on CBS Morning News and on National Public Radio, and we got a tremendous amount of media attention for this book. We sold around sixty thousand copies before I licensed the book (and two other books in the series) to a big New York publisher. I'm prouder of that book than anything we've done, because it had the greatest chance to fail completely. After all, the authors were nineteen years old, and it was kind of a weird idea. Most college prep books are written by adults who've had twenty years in educational counseling. It was an unusual idea that worked.

□ How do publishers differentiate themselves?

Publishers—especially small publishers—tend to develop a list that feeds off itself. That means when you sell one book you can say, "Hey, we've got another book that's somewhat similar, either in the category or style or topic." In other words, you don't want to just scatter-shot and publish one New Age book on crystals and then a first novel and then a travel guide to New York City. You want to develop a niche, so booksellers can know in four or five seconds what your company is all about.

□ What do you look for in a book proposal?

The first thing I look for is, Does this proposal fit our niche? One thing I like to see in proposals is a familiarity with the books that we've published.

Then, since I'm the one who's going to be editing the book and working with the author for as long as it takes, I have to be personally interested in the topic. It's got to spark my curiosity.

Then I look to see what else on the market is similar.

Does the book have an easily targeted market? For example, it can't be just be some "guide for men." You're not going to have 125 million men walking into the bookstore buying that book. It's got to focus on a market.

I look at whether it can be produced within a certain budget so that I can make a profit off it.

All of those things go into the decision to consider a book. If you tell me the title of the book, I'm thinking of all those things.

If that hurdle is cleared, I look at how the cover letter and proposal are written. Is the grammar good? Is it easy and interesting to read? Does it lure me into the proposal? Is everything spelled properly?

A woman once sent me a book proposal—a guide to household poisons. She misspelled the word "poison" throughout the entire proposal—POSION!

It might have been a good book, but she had no credibility.

□ What should a complete book proposal include?

I generally like to see a cover letter, an outline, and two or three sample chapters. And a self-addressed, stamped envelope is an absolute must.

□ Are you looking at an author's writing style in the query letter and the proposal?

Very much. But only after it has passed those initial hurdles. Usually, books don't.

□ How long does it take you to make a decision on a proposal?

It depends on the proposal, and it depends on the list that I'm developing for the next season. If the book is going to fit a certain niche within that list, then I might act more quickly or delay it for a season. Some books are seasonal in nature. You probably want to publish travel guides in the spring. You want to publish test prep and college application type books in the fall.

□ **How much input do you give once the contract is signed and the writing procedure starts?**

It depends how far the author is into the book. Sometimes I get a query on just an idea for a book, and then I can have a lot of input. If the query is for a finished manuscript, obviously the book is pretty well done already.

With a company this size, I'm getting proposals from authors who might have a great deal of knowledge in a particular field, but they're not necessarily writers. They're depending on me to make the manuscript resemble the English language. They can get all the information and organize it to appeal to their particular audience. But a lot of times, polishing the writing is my job.

□ **What about phone calls from writers?**

I hate phone calls from writers about book proposals. I'm not interviewing applicants for a radio DJ job. I don't need to hear their voice. I'm interviewing applicants for a writing job. I need to see how they write. If somebody calls up and says, "I've got this idea for a book," if it's nonfiction, I usually say, "That sounds like something I might like to take a look at—send it to me." You just wasted two or three minutes of my time and your phone call. If I have to answer the phone all day about book proposals, I'll never get any real work done. With the mail, I can do it on my own time. And I try to respond to all queries promptly—within two to three weeks.

□ **Do you have words to the wise for authors who are seeking a publisher?**

I think persistence is the main thing. If you believe strongly enough in your idea, then don't take rejection from publishers A, B, and C personally. They just might not be the right publishers for your idea. There are thousands of publishing companies in this country now. In fact, the major growth area of publishing in the last ten years has been small presses.

If you are so determined and so convinced that there is a market for your book, then there's probably a publisher for it. It's a matter of persisting until you find the right publisher at the right time.

□ **Do you have words of warning for writers?**

Don't have false expectations. I find that writers hear about John Grisham making $30 million or Norman Mailer getting a $12 million advance. And they think, "Well, I'm not Norman Mailer, but I could probably get a $1 million advance." Sure—and I'll be nominated for a Pulitzer Prize next year.

There are all kinds of depressing statistics around. A common one is "Three out of five books lose money, one book breaks even, and one book makes a lot of money."

Nobody is in this business to get rich. Very few people have gotten rich in this business.

□ Why write a book, if not for money?

Write a book, not because you want to make $1 million, but because you have a personal vision and a statement, and you want to undertake the creative challenge of writing a book and having it published. If you make money off the deal, then that's just icing. But don't expect to make a dime.

There are fifty thousand new books published every year. How many books did you read last year? And how many of those books were new? If you read ten books, I bet five of them were published three years ago—or maybe a hundred years ago.

18

The Medium-Size Press

MIKE URBAN, EDITORIAL DIRECTOR
The Globe Pequot Press, Inc.
Old Saybrook, Connecticut

MICHAEL URBAN'S first job was editorial assistant for a small medical publisher. He then went to Rand McNally for three years, World Books for four years, and National Textbook Company (NTC) for four more years, before accepting his present position as editorial director at Globe Pequot (since 1991). His specialty is travel editing.

Globe Pequot began in the 1940s as the Stonington Press, a publisher of local town histories. An advertising executive purchased the company in the early 1970s and renamed it the Pequot Press. After ten years, the company was acquired by the *Boston Globe*. It is now a subsidiary of AT&T Wireless.

Globe Pequot Press is a medium-size publisher with five full-time staff editors. Most of the paper and pencil editing is done by outside free-lancers. The nonfiction list includes travel, outdoor recreation, gardening, cooking, nature, family activities, and personal finance. Their unofficial slogan is "Books for the good life."

Globe Pequot publishes 30 to 40 new titles each year, 150 total books including imports and revisions, and receives 400 submissions annually.

☐ **How do you usually acquire your books?**
There are three ways we sign up books: from proposals sent primarily from agents; from the slush pile; and from internally generated ideas. It's about 30 percent agented and 70 percent nonagented. We read everything that comes in

over the transom. If you don't have an agent, that doesn't count against you. An unagented author has just as good a chance.

□ **What are the advantages and disadvantages of your location outside New York City?**
We're at an advantage in that things are a little more sane here. We're at a disadvantage because agents can't knock on the door as easily as they can in New York.

I don't really think our location hurts us. It attracts some attention. Many people find that going to a smaller house outside New York breaks some of the molds. We give a little more specialized attention and treatment to the authors and agents. We get plenty of material.

□ **Why would an author want to work with a medium-size publisher?**
The biggest advantage is that you're going to get more specialized attention. If you're at a bigger house, chances are you won't get as much attention as you would from somebody like us. There isn't a revolving door in terms of employment here, so the editor you start with, 95 percent of the time, is the editor you'll finish with on the project. That person will take a lot of personal care of your book. There will be a lot of back and forth. Our authors are queried on the manuscript, see galleys, see page proofs. They're brought all the way down the line.

□ **What kinds of attention will you give an author that he or she may not receive at a large house?**
Probably most important is the publicity and promotion side. People like to publish with us because they're going to have a better chance of leading the parade, a better chance for recognition, of being a top author. If an author publishes with a large house, where they're doing five hundred books a year, he may get lost in the shuffle.

□ **What about the disadvantages of signing a contract with a medium-size publisher?**
You'll probably make more money with a bigger house. Our advances—depending on the book, range from $1,500 to $7,500. We do go into five figures, but it's rare. We will do it for the right book.

□ **What are the advantages for the author of working with a medium-size publisher compared to a tiny publisher, who publishes only five books a year?**
We can offer what bigger publishers do—good, solid, nation-wide distribution. We use a commissioned rep force, who carry our books, as well as a half-dozen other publishers' books, throughout the country. We have two in-house people

who do nothing but work on national accounts—Barnes & Noble, Walden Books, Baker & Taylor, and so forth. We also have a special sales manager who handles book club sales, and who recently signed up a nation-wide group of commissioned gift store reps.

□ **What about media coverage after the book is published?**

We have a three-person publicity department. They get a lot of positive print coverage for our books, and they get our authors on nation-wide and local radio and television talk shows. We don't give the same sort of media attention to every book, but we can give more attention to each individual title. Large companies have much more muscle, power, and money, but they tend to focus on their top two or three books. The other two hundred or three hundred don't get that sort of attention.

□ **What do you look for in a proposal?**

The author should know what we publish and present a proposal that blends with our list. The author should know there's a certain niche that hasn't been covered or a certain angle on a topic that no one else has covered before. A good proposal is neat, organized, and concise. It should have a short cover letter describing what the book is, a one- or two-page outline stating what the book purports to be, the potential audience for the book, a table of contents, and the author's credentials for writing the book. Credentials are important because we like to publicize authors as experts in whatever it is they're writing about.

The shorter, the better, with a proposal. If we like what we see, we can go back and ask for more.

□ **Do you ever want an entire manuscript?**

We don't want entire manuscripts. We don't even need a half-dozen sample chapters.

□ **Do authors ever do the wrong thing and annoy you?**

Yes. We're frequently annoyed by prospective authors.

Don't call on the phone with a book idea and gab for five or ten minutes about what your book is and how great it is. We don't want to hear about your book; we want to read about it. Books are written documents. You've got to show us on paper that you can write well and present your ideas well.

□ **Can an author feel assured that the query letter and proposal will be read?**

Yes. It takes time, anywhere from twenty-four hours to two to three months. For those in the slush pile, it can be four months. You'll hear back quickly if your book is one of two things. If it's something that we're very excited about and we're immediately interested in, you'll probably hear back within twenty-four to forty-eight hours. For the book that we're definitely not interested in, you'll hear back within a couple of weeks.

If it's something that we're sort of interested in, but we're not sure, you might wait for two to four months. It will be in limbo. We have to go to sales and marketing and ask, "Would you like a book like this?"

☐ **Do you have words to the wise for authors in search of a publisher?**
Think of the kind of book you want to do. Target the publishers in that area. Get a copy of the publishers' catalogs. Study their lists. See what they're doing. Go to a bookstore and look through some of the books they've published. Narrow it down to two or three publishers that look particularly appealing. When you enter the game, just like in a job interview, you know who the publishers are and what they do, and you have a game plan for how you can write a book that will enhance their list.

First-time authors should go for smaller houses rather than bigger houses. As a rule, you have a better chance of getting published with a smaller house. Big houses just don't have time. They're flooded with proposals. It's hard for them to get through their material.

19

The Megapublisher

DEB BRODY, SENIOR EDITOR
Dutton Signet
Division of Penguin USA
New York

DEB BRODY majored in journalism in college, but opted for a career in publishing rather than writing. After graduation, she worked as an editorial assistant in the New York office of Contemporary Books, and went to Facts on File and then to HarperCollins as associate editor before landing a position at Dutton Signet as editor. She was promoted to senior editor a year later. Brody edits only nonfiction. Her list includes books on health, parenting, psychology, sports, careers, and biographies. She does not edit business, politics, or New Age books.

Penguin USA is the umbrella company of Dutton Signet and one of the largest publishing houses in the world. The company is divided into two major subsidiaries: Viking/Penguin (Viking publishes hardcover; Penguin publishes trade paperback) and Dutton Signet (Signet is the mass market line; Dutton is hardcover). Other imprints include Plume, a trade paperback line; Roc, a science fiction line; Topaz, a romance imprint; and Viking Studio, highly illustrated books.

Dutton Signet publishes about 360 books annually and receives more than ten times as many proposals.

☐ **How do you usually acquire books?**
I would say 95 percent of what I do, and most other editors here as well, is through agents. If we like something, we bring it up at a weekly editorial meeting. All of the editors and the publisher attend this meeting.

□ **How do you decide whether a book fits into your publishing program?**
You hope that agents know you and send you things that are right for your list. Part of the job is to get to know agents and let them know what it is that you personally as an editor do or the company does so they're not wasting their time or your time by sending you the wrong things. If a really great proposal doesn't fit in, we sometimes send it to another division. We often send it back to the agent saying, "This doesn't work for us. If you want to, send it someplace else."

□ **Do you ever compete with other divisions of your huge company?**
At the same time that we cooperate with Viking/Penguin, we often compete with them. Agents will often send the same proposal to an editor here and to an editor at another Viking/Penguin imprint.

□ **Is a writer better off going with a big publisher?**
I think the advantages probably outweigh the disadvantages. The advantages are mostly distribution—a sales force that can get the books into the stores.

On the publicity end, because we do major books, we have contacts with major media, whether it is television or print media.

□ **Can a writer expect a larger advance with big publisher?**
Yes, although not necessarily. The money can be a selling point. We offer anything from $3,000 to six figures. Quite varied.

□ **What about different types of books and the advantages and disadvantages between smaller and larger publishers?**
It's important that writers look at who publishes similar books. Certain books can be done very well by small houses and others can't. It depends on what outlets you want, especially if you have the kind of book that can be sold in places other than bookstores. We get into special markets, because we have a special sales department, where we sell to corporations and to catalogs and things like that. If your book lends itself to that, you'd be better off with a large publisher.

Certain travel books, for example, can be done very well with small regional publishers who do only one thing and do it well.

Because we do so much and certain books have to take precedence, smaller books tend to get lost. When you publish thirty or more books a season, you can't give equal time to all thirty or fifty or one hundred books.

□ **How do you decide whether it is a "small" book or a "large" book?**
It's based on the first print run, which is based on the perceived market. Certain books will automatically be small—very literary novels tend to be smaller than big commercial novels. You're going to put much more money into a big com-

mercial novel, meaning more advertising, more publicity money, a bigger tour. It has nothing to do with the quality of the book. It's just the number of people who are going to read it.

□ **Do you tell the author up front, while you're negotiating the contract, whether the book is considered "small" or "large"?**
It's not always clear at that point. When you negotiate a book, you don't know exactly what will happen with it.

□ **How do you view "small" books and "large" books?**
I consider a small book backlist rather than frontlist. I mean, you go out there and sell it as a frontlist book, but you hope that it sells for years and years to come. Like a lot of parenting books, things like that. Fiction is frontlist, usually. With fiction, you go out there and try to sell fifty thousand copies up front.

□ **What do you want included in a proposal for a nonfiction book?**
The most important thing is that the writer has thought out the whole book. That would be evident in the proposal. What I like to see is either a table of contents or a chapter outline, a sample chapter, and an analysis of the market and an analysis of the competition. An author must show how his or her book will be different and/or better than what's out there. An author biography should be included. If the author has written another book, he or she should include either a copy of the previous book or reviews of the book, if it was well received.

I look for credentials in an author of a nonfiction book, especially in areas that are very crowded, like parenting and health. You have to have a name or the credentials that will stand out. That's one of the most important things I look for. Even if I see a great proposal, I will often dismiss something by someone who doesn't have the credentials. It doesn't seem fair, but it's a very competitive market and in terms of selling, credentials help. I rarely look at a health book that doesn't have an M.D. attached to it.

□ **What about proposals for fiction?**
Fiction is almost always bought on a full manuscript.

□ **How long does it take for you to make a decision on a proposal?**
It can take as little as a week, if you get something in that you're very excited about, that's very hot, that a lot of other people are going to be seeing and bidding on. It can also take many, many months.

□ **Tell me about the distribution process of a big company like Penguin.**
We have a sales force—a paperback sales force and a hardcover sales force. Sales reps go out and sell to the independent bookstores. We also sell directly to the

wholesalers, from which bookstores can order. And we sell directly to the major chains.

□ Do you have pet peeves about authors?

A lot of it is just personality, whether you click with somebody. That's going to happen in any working relationship, no matter what industry you're in. I certainly understand and appreciate authors who are concerned about their book and want to know what's going on. There's a fine line between being concerned and being a pest. It's when authors call every day, and assume that their book is the only book the editor is working on, that it gets to be a little much.

□ Do you think that authors who pester you are afraid that their book is being shoved out?

No. It happens at all levels. Every editor will tell you that. It doesn't matter about the size of the book. It's hard to disagree or to not understand why somebody is doing this. Every book is important, especially to the author. But, as an editor, as I'm working on thirty books at a time, I can't have thirty authors calling me every day.

□ Do you have words to the wise for authors who are in search of a publisher?

Get an agent. That's the first step, for two reasons.

First, as an editor, I look at agented submissions first, and I put unagented submissions at the bottom of the pile.

Second, if you have an agent, an editor knows that the proposal has been through at least one filter. A good agent will work with an author to get a very good proposal. The chances of getting it published are infinitely greater.

20

University Presses

LINDSAY WATERS

EXECUTIVE EDITOR FOR THE HUMANITIES

Harvard University Press
Cambridge, Massachusetts

LINDSAY WATERS, Executive Editor of Harvard University Press, graduated from college with a degree in English. After earning his Ph.D. in English and Italian, he taught humanities and writing at Chicago State University and the University of Minnesota. Lindsay "jumped ship" in 1978 to join the University of Minnesota Press, where he climbed the ranks to editor in chief. In 1984 he went to Harvard University Press as a general editor. His editing specialties are philosophy and literature.

Harvard University Press publishes about 120 new hardcover books a year. They receive thousands of proposals annually. "We are just bombarded," says Waters.

□ **When did university presses come into existence?**
They came into existence in the English-speaking world five or six hundred years ago. The development of the printing press went hand in hand with the translation of the Bible into all the tongues of Europe and its dissemination, with the rediscovery of ancient texts and their dissemination, and with the development of humanistic forms of education.

□ **What purpose did university presses originally serve?**
They served as printers for Bibles and for works of scholarship about the Bible back when scholars were more religious, tied to a more monastic way of life.

In the late nineteenth century, when the German model of graduate education took root in the English-speaking world, first at Johns Hopkins, then at the University of Chicago, Harvard, the University of California, and elsewhere, there was a new notion that teachers ought to be producing scholarship and writing and publishing books. To be a scholar was not just to teach people or have ideas, but to get those ideas down on paper and communicate them by that method.

□ How did university presses fit into the universities at that time?
At the beginning, in the 1890s, the presses were basically parts of the printing departments of the universities or attached to the libraries. Books would often circulate among the universities. For example, the University of Chicago library would swap books with the Heidelberg University library.

□ When did the university presses become more professional?
After World War II, academic university presses became proper publishing houses. Some major figures came to the university presses from New York publishing houses with lots of experience, not just in printing and swapping, but actually publishing books and getting them out to the public. Roger Shugg, from Knopf, was the founder of the modern University of Chicago Press. The presses all became more professional and began the process of evaluating their books as a way of selecting them that has remained one of the hallmarks of university press publication.

□ What was the result of this evaluation of books?
The presses became better publishers, better distributors, and better publicists, and academic standards rose. University presses would no longer publish books just because they were written by their faculty. They would publish books by any intellectuals—such as mavericks like Kenneth Burke and Paul Goodman—if they could meet standards of quality.

□ What purpose do university presses serve today?
Their basic job is to convey knowledge from scholars to other scholars and to students throughout the world. Some university presses in the United States are the major publishing house in their region of the country. More than just conveying knowledge, the presses have a role in challenging scholars to develop new and different ideas.

□ Give me an example of university presses that function as a region's major publishing house.
Louisiana State University Press, University of Arizona Press, and University of New Mexico Press are examples.

□ **How do these university presses serve the community as well as the university?**

The university press can be part of an outreach program to bring ideas to a wider public. They extend the home university, allowing it to operate far from home base. They connect their faculty with the international community of scholars, but they also serve the nonscholarly community by publishing books about, for example, the architecture of Chicago or the architecture of the upper Midwest or Cajun music. The Minnesota Press has scholars who produce lively presentations of the geology of Minnesota. Why does this interesting state have such strange and unusual geology? The Press will help geologists write books and give them feedback so those ideas and that knowledge can reach as many people as possible. A press like Minnesota or Arizona or Nebraska may become a major publisher of the work of native Americans, whether that work takes the form of history or fiction.

□ **Are some university presses now similar to commercial publishers?**

Some people think that's the case. I don't think so. The university press tries to serve God and mammon simultaneously, performing a complex juggling act. The job of the commercial house is to serve mammon alone.

□ **Do university presses ever publish blockbusters?**

Of course there are blockbusters. But those often arise in a very natural way from publishers doing a good job in bringing complex, intellectual, academic ideas out to the public. One of our blockbusters has sold over a half-million copies. That book arose because good editors were keeping their ears to the ground, heard about this interesting specialized scholarship, saw those sparks, and started fanning them. But a half-million of Carol Gilligan's *In a Different Voice* is a far cry from the sales of a Stephen King novel.

□ **Is a blockbuster from a university press more literary or of higher quality than one from a trade publisher?**

We wouldn't say that we are more holy and other publishers are barbarians. The imprint of the university is always involved, so there is quality control. I just don't think it helps much to speak about blockbusters in the world of university presses. We don't have them in the normal sense of the word.

□ **How do university presses differ from trade publishers?**

We're not absolutely different in the sense that all of us and some of them are trying to get ideas across to people. University presses can and must live with lower sales. Our raison d'être is not the bottom line. We might be happy with a book that sells as few as three hundred or five hundred copies a year, as long as it keeps chugging along. We might even be proud of doing a book that only sells six hundred copies, if it's a crucial book that might still be in print twenty or thirty years from now. We wouldn't survive if that's all we did. But if someone gives us the most spectacular, absolutely first-rate book that's ever been written about a particular book in the Hebrew Bible, and it's only going to sell a few hundred copies, we're going to do it.

□ How do university presses usually acquire their books?
The same way all publishers acquire books. We take in our mail; we throw it out. And then we go out on to the highways and byways looking for authors. Good editors build up networks of advisors. Everybody in publishing does this to some extent. We do it more in the sense that we want to be our own agents. Editors in university publishing have more leeway and responsibility than those in trade houses. All editors hustle. We check and see who's winning Guggenheims and other grants. Who is going to interesting conferences? We write to them, go to the conferences ourselves, visit university campuses, visit authors, use the telephone all the time. When I first started working in publishing at the University of Minnesota Press, I think my phone bill was higher than my salary.

□ Do you deal with agents?
Yes. But it is really limited. As I said, we want to be our own agents. We want to be in charge. We don't want to, nor can we be, paying huge finder's fees. We don't want to buy high and sell high.

□ What kind of books are you looking for?
We're looking for a range of nonfiction works, books that are in it for the long haul. We're looking for books in the humanities and social sciences, for history books, and increasingly for science books. We're hungry for new ideas.

□ Do your authors need credentials?
They don't need credentials. We're interested in writers who are pushing the frontiers of what can be said about things. In a way, we're an extension and a development of the university, a kind of a outreach program. Many authors outside the academy have very important educational lessons for people inside the academy.

□ How many university presses exist in the United States and how many books do they publish?
I am quoting from the American Association of University Presses (AAUP), which lists all of the presses, addresses, and names of the major editors. The 109 members of the AAUP annually publish nearly eight thousand books and more than five hundred periodicals. In fact, a major job of university presses is publishing journals.

□ Are university presses profit-making?

Sometimes they make a profit. We do better than break even, but we are always sailing close to the wind. Some presses are maintained with university subsidies, but no press will be tolerated or carried along for long if it's running deficits or going beyond what has been allocated as a subsidy. More university presses than you would expect don't receive subsidy and have to make it on what they earn. The main thing is to keep afloat, but also move forward. It is a challenging action sport. Really.

□ Is the implication that writers probably earn less money from a book that is published by a university press?

No. The university press is not a charity, a sort of blood bank to which an author gives his blood. We do different sorts of books that have different sorts of sales lives. For most of our books we are much more apt to assure an author of royalty income. There are odd and unusual books where a trade house might do as well or slightly worse than us because we are set up to reach a mix of intellectuals and academics and students through bookstores and direct mail and because we keep a book in print over an extended period. When we signed up one of our major books, New York houses were offering twice the advance we were offering. The book was a complicated, intellectual, interesting one that needed special treatment. The writer's agent thought it might have been held quite well by some of the New York publishers. She wasn't quite sure why the author wanted to go with a university press. After the first year's royalties came in, the agent apologized.

□ Why would a writer want to be published by a university press?

We can make a well-written academic book reach a wider audience by allowing it to catch on among the members of that talkative little club called the academic world first. As you know, word of mouth is really the best advertisement for any book, but you cannot buy it. There are three things money cannot buy: home grown tomatoes, love, and word-of-mouth advertising. We go to meetings, we direct-mail books to different kinds of audiences, and we have large lists of book buyers that we have built up ourselves and we can rent lists. If the book is tricky in any way, a university press might do a better job with it. I think of our books *Lipstick Traces* by Greil Marcus and *The Alchemy of Race and Rights* by Patricia Williams.

□ Some authors think that, in negotiating a contract, the bottom line of a book's ultimate success is the advance.

I think that's a real mistake. "By their fruit ye shall judge them." Take a look in the bookstores. Whose books are selling? What is the reputation of the publisher with bookstores?

Some publishers pay a large advance. Perhaps the author should just run with it and not worry about whether the book gets well-distributed and well-publicized. But that is short-sighted.

Who is publishing the books that *you* read? It is much better to be guided by that. Putting money down on the line is a certain form of commitment. But beware: it may mean that the publisher needs you more than you need them. You can be misled. The highest bidder is not necessarily the best publisher.

□ What is the range of advances that you offer?

Our job is not to have a whole bunch of money out in advances. That's not what we're supposed to do. We might pay $10,000 or $20,000 for a book that we could publish wonderfully. If another publisher would pay $100,000 for the same book, we would congratulate the author. We have to husband our resources. We don't have large cash flows. Our money is not our own. It belongs to the university. We have to be very careful, but that doesn't mean we should pass up opportunities.

□ What is the standard royalty offered by university presses?

I don't think there is a standard royalty. They usually begin at 10 percent on the net price for hardcover and 7.5 percent of net for paperback, moving up to list-based royalties for genuine trade books.

□ How does a proposal or manuscript win approval at a university press?

First, it gets read by the editor. We present proposals to our in-house editorial committee, which looks at publishing and scholarly questions. We will have a finished manuscript reviewed by a couple of scholars. There's often negotiation between the editor and the author about revisions. We take the revised manuscript to the faculty board. Every press has a faculty board that has the final say. The boards are always concerned about merit, not about publishing issues. Then the book is approved or not approved.

□ What do you want included in an outstanding proposal?

A chapter outline. A good sense of how a book fits into the existing literature. The proposal should be well written. It shouldn't be too long.

□ What do you advise authors in search of a university publisher?

Learn about publishers as humans with careers like yours. What have they done in the last three years? Get the catalogs. Talk to people in bookstores. Look at your own shelves. Whose books are you buying? Whose books are you reading?

Try to find the right editor, somebody committed to your field. You may see acknowledgments to a particular editor at a certain publishing house. You may see that name appear repeatedly in books you have liked. That's a sign. Think of the publisher like you think of yourself: as a person with predilections. Some publishers are proud to say they publish authors, not books. What should that relationship look like from an author's point of view? Publish with an editor, not a book manufacturer. Think of your own work not rigidly, but flexibly, as something that might be shaped and reshaped to best challenge and win over readers. Have fun!

21

Canadian Publishing

PHYLLIS BRUCE, PUBLISHER AND
EDITOR-AT-LARGE
Phyllis Bruce Books
Imprint of HarperCollins Publishers Ltd
Toronto

PHYLLIS BRUCE was an English major in college. After graduation, she taught high school English, then went into educational publishing. After five years, she switched to trade publishing. In 1991 Bruce left her position as editor in chief of Key Porter Books to set up her own imprint at HarperCollins, Canada. Her editing specialty is Canadian studies.

Phyllis Bruce Books publishes six to eight books a year—books that are mostly Bruce's ideas. She creates the projects, finds the authors, and the books come out under her name. Phyllis Bruce books are sold as part of the larger HarperCollins Canadian program.

HarperCollins Canada is a combination of Harper and Row, U.S., and Collins, U.K, a fusion of American and British agencies in Canada. HarperCollins Canada is one the five largest trade publishers in Canada.

□ **How does Canadian publishing differ from publishing in other countries?**
The market in Canada is much smaller. The Canadian publishing program has to struggle to find its place in the face of really big titles coming in from other countries. It's a sandwich situation in terms of developing a publishing program here. Another way Canadian publishing is different is that our market is further divided in Canada because we have a French market. Canadian publishers are

occasionally attracted to books that have a French potential. Our choice of books may be affected by whether we can sell rights to a publisher in Quebec.

□ How do Canadian publishers compete?
The issue is the market and what sells in Canada. You obviously can't compete with really big titles from other countries head on. So you try to develop Canadian titles that have their own unique market here, or you tend to buy rights to the other books coming into the Canadian market. For example, Canadian rights are bought by a company here for John Irving's books and John Irving is treated as our author.

□ How many people in Canada buy books?
There are about 27 million people in Canada. About 20 million buy books.

□ Is Canadian publishing subsidized or controlled by the government?
A publishing company must have at least 75 percent Canadian ownership to receive government subsidies, which come from the federal and provincial levels and apply to publisher and writers. Companies without the 75 percent ownership qualification do not get money.

□ How do government subsidies make publishing different from companies that do not receive them—different from American publishing?
I think the question is, "Does it make them better publishers because they're getting government money?" No. The money is provided to counteract the size of the market. In the long run, the money enables publishers to survive in the face of overseas competition.

Government money enhances our effectiveness in the international market. It's not just for direct publishing of books. It assists publishers in trade development and international marketing by subsidizing foreign travel to book fares, trade shows, and the like. Canadian publishers have been more successful in the international market in the past ten years than they were before they had government assistance. The domestic market usually goes toward the bottom line of the Canadian publishing company.

□ How do authors apply and qualify for government assistance?
The authors apply and the publisher makes a recommendation.

□ Are there differences between the federal and the provincial systems?
There is a difference between how the systems work at the federal and provincial levels.

The federal level has a competition by the jury system. The author completes and submits the forms, and gets a publisher to verify that he or she is a good writer.

At the provincial level, each publishing house that qualifies is given a certain amount of money. Writers apply to the publisher for support. The publisher can allot a certain amount of money to a project up to a certain point. It varies slightly from province to province. Not every province has writers' grants. Some of the larger provinces have grants and the smaller provinces don't.

□ **Do Canadian writers go to American publishers?**
A Canadian author would love to get into the U.S. market because it's so much larger. But it's hard to get the attention of a U.S. publisher if you're a Canadian writer, unless you have international stature.

□ **Can American book writers get published in Canada?**
Yes, if they have an idea that appeals. There are two ways that American writers can get into the Canadian market: (1) if they're so well known that a Canadian house will want to buy the rights; or (2) if they have a book with Canadian content or on a subject that would be of interest to Canadians. It can be fiction or nonfiction. The American authors I've worked with have been writing out of Canada. That is the easiest way to get in.

□ **Are there barriers between the two countries that would create writing problems for Americans?**
Yes. The legal system is different. The medical system is different. These differences would come into play if you are writing nonfiction.

□ **If an American writer wants to write a book about a Canadian subject—fishing in Canadian lakes, for example—should he or she or the agent go to a Canadian publisher or to an American publisher?**
He or his agent should go to a Canadian publisher or go to an American publisher who is close to Canada and publishes books about fishing in Canada because people in that area fish in Canada. Some regional American publishers copublish with Canada because there's a band that runs through the two countries. The climate is the same. They buy Canadian gardening books, for example, and Canadian publishers buy American gardening books.

The better qualified you are and the more credibility you have, the better chance you have of getting across the border into Canada. The question arises, "Why buy a book from an American author? There's somebody here who could write that book as well. That person would be more accessible for promotion, so why shouldn't I just get a Canadian writer to do this book on fly fishing, rather than an American?"

□ **Are book contracts different in the two countries?**
Publishing contracts in Canada are almost identical to publishing contracts in the States. The legal differences between the two countries wouldn't affect a publishing contract. There are different libel laws. The warrantee clause is worded slightly differently from country to country. I negotiate contracts with U.S. writers just the way I do with Canadian writers. If he has an agent, I work through the agent or I work with the writer.

□ **Will most Canadian publishers deal with unagented writers?**
Most Canadian publishers will no longer take unsolicited fiction. The smaller publishers will, but the larger publishers won't. It's a bit more flexible for nonfiction. For one thing, you're not getting the whole manuscript to read. You're just getting a proposal.

□ **What do you want in a book proposal?**
I want a thoughtful outline of the content, and some sample writing. The writing doesn't necessarily have to be from the proposal itself, though that would help. In the case of fiction, I have to see the whole manuscript. I want the author's credentials for the book, why the author thinks the book will sell, and the market for the book. Although I have a lot of control over my imprint, I work with a publishing committee and must present projects for discussion and approval. The author must convince publishing and marketing people on the basis of six or seven pages. If the proposal is not well written, if it doesn't have a clear focus, if the author doesn't appear to have done the job, then it's doomed from the beginning.

In the last year or so everybody's faxing everything. An unsolicited fax proposal does not make a good impression with a publishing company, particular, long, unsolicited proposals. Faxing a proposal is a very bad way to introduce yourself to a publishing company. It's not a good idea unless the author has been asked to do it or the writer knows the publisher well.

□ **What do you want in a book proposal from an American writer?**
It helps if the American submitting the proposal knows about the Canadian market, particularly for nonfiction. I'm really impressed by proposals that show that the writer has gone into a bookstore, has looked at competition, knows what's out there, and has some sense of the market.

□ **How long does a decision take after you receive a proposal?**
Two to three weeks.

□ **What is the range of advances that you offer authors?**
Our advances range from $3,000 to $200,000. The advance system is exactly the same as the U.S. system. It's contingent on the projected sales of the book, the importance of the author, and so on. Royalties are also identical.

□ What kind of money do authors of blockbusters earn?

Canadian writers have made over a $1 million on books. The Canadian writers who make the most money are usually published internationally—people like Margaret Atwood, who get a three- or four-way publication on the first go on a novel. Some Canadian writers have made an enormous amount of money out of specialty markets like cookbooks, for example. The market is about a tenth the size of the States'. It scales down accordingly. Nevertheless, some Canadian authors have become quite wealthy.

□ What do you do for media promotion?

Everything. Radio, television, space advertising, magazine advertising, author tours. There's less national media here that we can plug into. Personal author appearances—readings and signings—are really important. Not that they aren't on the States' side. But we don't have national talk shows the way you do. The most effective way to sell books in Canada is radio, whereas in the States it would be television. If Canadian writers ever get on Oprah Winfrey or Larry King, they think they've died and gone to heaven. The numbers are just unbelievable. To even get a reference on American television is just amazing.

We have to send our authors places. That's why an American author who isn't particularly famous will have a difficult time getting published in Canada. A Canadian publisher doesn't want to pay that person to come up here and travel across the country. The physical distance is important. It is a fair investment of money for a publisher to send an author to Vancouver and back.

□ Do you have pet peeves?

My major peeve is that authors sometimes don't tell me how bad things are. I have to rescue books in-house from marketing people, who say, "If it's late, it must be bad." The assumption on the marketing side is that if a book is late, it's not well written. That's not necessarily the case, but the assumption is made. If the book is canceled, it sends out a very bad message before the book even arrives. The publisher starts to slot the book into the system early on. In Canada, our machines turn over much more quickly than American publishers. We will get a manuscript in February, March, or April for fall publication.

The average lead time for Canadian publishers would be six to eight months. It's really important that authors level with publishers about whether they're going to be able to meet their manuscript deadlines because there's nothing worse than listing a book and finding out that there's no manuscript.

Missed deadlines can be really critical, particularly if you're at the point that promotional materials are being prepared and cataloging is taking place. If the publisher is to the point of cataloging the book and the author does not indicate that the manuscript is not available, then the book is catalogued and sold or canceled, as the case may be. A canceled book leaves a really bad impression with the marketing people, not to mention the bookstores.

□ **Do you have advice for American authors in search of a Canadian publisher?**

American writers should call two associations in Canada—the Association of Canadian Book Publishers (ACP) or the Canadian Book Publishers Council—to get advice on Canadian publishers and the Canadian market. That may be one way to target a Canadian publisher more precisely.

It might be helpful to get your hands on *The Globe and Mail* and look at the best-seller lists to see what's selling in the Canadian market.

Part Two

Specialized Books

22

Art and Illustrated Books

SUSAN R. COSTELLO, EDITORIAL DIRECTOR
Abbeville Press, Inc.
New York

SUSAN COSTELLO, Editorial Director, majored in Russian history in college. She was studying for her master's degree in history when she took a job as a secretary at Random House in New York. "This supposedly doesn't happen," says Costello, "but it did. When it was discovered that I couldn't type, I was promoted to be an editor. That was how my whole publishing career started—in 1962."

"Here's something else that editors don't do too often," she adds. "I transferred to magazines and worked for *Life* International as a researcher and reporter. Usually, you don't go from books to magazines."

After that, Costello freelanced. She then went back to book publishing. "I find that very well rounded," she explains. "These days people tend to specialize. In book publishing, people specialize in illustrated or nonillustrated, fiction or nonfiction. I found that moving back and forth was helpful for my career and also for my overview of publishing."

Costello was managing editor of Abbeville for three years before attaining her present position in 1992.

Abbeville Press was founded in 1977 by Robert E. Abrams with his father, the late Harry N. Abrams, who also founded Abrams Publishers. Costello refers to sixteen-year-old Abbeville as a "small to medium-size teenager."

Robert Abrams has been president since 1979. Abbeville publishes approximately fifty original books annually.

□ How do you usually acquire books?

Usually from our previously published authors or from ideas generated in-house. From other publishers or packagers, museums or galleries, and agents. Then, of course submissions from authors or photographers.

□ What makes a successful illustrated book?

The best illustrated books are ones that result from an intense collaboration between the writer and/or photographer and the editor. The designer and production people also contribute enormously to the final result.

If we let the author do what the author does best, and the designer do what the designer does best, and the editor and so on, and everyone specializes in their field of expertise, the book can be terrific.

□ What kind of readership do you focus on?

We look for an interesting subject with a potentially wide readership. A book that would appeal to the trade, but also to book clubs and non-trade book outlets, such as gift shops and museum shops.

Since we're an international publisher, we look for an international readership. All books may not appeal to that broad market. I'm envisioning the ideal book.

□ What should proposals for art and illustrated books include?

The proposal should be thoughtfully and creatively conceived.

Will pictures be supplied by the author? Is there going to be an author-photographer team? Does Abbeville have to gather the photos? (We have a photo research department, so we can do that with a detailed picture list supplied by the author.) What's the relationship between the text and the photos?

What is the competition in terms of the editorial concept and the price point? How is the book different from the competition?

Is the author promotable? This may also determine whether we take on a project. The author is another important part of the proposal.

□ Who would be the ideal author for you?

The ideal author is able to produce an authoritative text and also has a lively writing style. A journalist who is an expert is the perfect author. The author should not only be knowledgeable, but passionate or enthusiastic about the subject.

For example, we published a book on global warming with the Museum of National History and the Environmental Defense Fund. The author, Andrew Revkin, is just that ideal author. He is a journalist but he is also very knowledgeable about the subject. He was totally devoted to the subject and an engaging speaker.

Another ideal author is a celebrity, who may not be an expert about a subject but is willing to collaborate with a first-rate author. We published *The Art of Arousal* with Dr. Ruth Westheimer. She collaborated with a museum curator.

□ What, specifically, should the ideal proposal consist of?

There should be a summary of the concept. The table of contents should be annotated, if possible, because that's helpful in amplifying the subject. A sample chapter should be included, if it's available, and a sample of the pictorial material. Originals aren't necessary, duplicates are fine, in fact. We don't want to be responsible for originals. We also want a survey of the competition, including the book title, the publisher, the format, and the price. We also need information about when the text will be available—the schedule. When the picture list will be ready or when the pictures will provided.

□ Are your books translated?

Yes. We have an office in Paris. The books that would be suitable for a French audience, we do ourselves. Sometimes we may do a book in several languages at once, for example, French, German, and Japanese.

□ Does that affect the author's contract?

Yes. If it's an esoteric subject, say wallpaper and the artist, we might not do the book at all if there weren't an international audience.

Even though the English printing will be small, the book becomes attractive and doable if it will be bolstered by foreign editions.

We did *The Art of Arousal* with Dr. Ruth in several languages. The English edition was going to be large to begin with. The foreign editions made the publishing of this book even more attractive.

□ Is it more difficult to work with illustrated books?

Illustrated books are the most difficult books to reduce. Considering the book's varied elements—text, captions, front and back matter including notes, bibliographies, and so forth—it's very tricky handling all the stages. Everything has to be very carefully thought through.

□ Is it more expensive to produce illustrated books?

There's a big difference between our books and generic illustrated books. Abbeville is known for high-quality publications. We are likely to use heavy, expensive paper, such as hundred-pound paper. Sometimes we use an even more weighty paper. Our printing and binding are also top-quality. We put more money in the production end of it.

□ Do you consider your books artifacts?

If the definition of an artifact is something that's representative of a particular culture or stage of technological development (I'm reading from the dictionary),

I would say yes. If you define artifact as "usually inferior artistic work or mass-produced item," I would say no.

□ **Do your authors receive media coverage?**

Yes. Before the books are released we start to promote them. They are presented at our sales conference. The sales reps go out and take orders. After the books are published, we have a very active promotion and publicity department. We arrange interviews in all media, copies are sent to key reviewers, and the authors are signed up for lectures at clubs, museums, and bookstores.

□ **Is the relationship between the author and the editor very important?**

Yes. Illustrated books depend on cooperation between the publisher and the author or photographer. It's really teamwork. You could think of an illustrated book as a play or a film. The star players are the publisher, the author, and the photographer. There is also a supporting cast. If the star players all contribute constructively toward the production of the book and have the same goals in mind, the book evolves in a positive direction. The best books do evolve, and are hammered in stone at the proposal stage. A book progresses as an author's creative input merges with the publisher's and the photographer's.

□ **What are some author behaviors that you don't appreciate?**

Authors who are rigid about their ideas or unwilling to listen to suggestions on how to improve the text or design. Because books do evolve, they may take a long time to produce. I don't appreciate impatient authors.

The author's book is the most important item on that individual's agenda. But authors have to understand that they have a different agenda than editors. Editors have many books to develop at once. Eventually, the editor will spend an enormous amount of time and concentration on the individual's book when it is scheduled and it's time to work on that book.

□ **How do you feel about putting so much work into the book, when the author, not the editor, earns the royalty?**

Sometimes I believe the royalty should be shared. In illustrated books, the editor contributes an enormous amount of energy and ideas to a project.

□ **Will a rigid author hurt the book's chance for success?**

If the author imposes restrictions on the editor and on the designer, then the book may be inferior, and certainly may be less successful than a book benefiting from a dedicated team effort.

□ **Are multiple submissions okay?**

I appreciate it when a writer tells us it is a multiple submission, or that it's not a multiple submission, and the writer says, for example, "I need to know within three weeks, or I'm going to submit this to other publishers." I think that's fair. The publisher and the writer should be as open as possible—that's mutually beneficial.

Naturally, it's much nicer to know that one publisher is the only publisher an author is sending a proposal to. You feel more comfortable with that author. If a subject is very timely, and an author has to get that book done, it's understandable why there would be multiple submissions.

□ **Do most of your authors have agents?**
Some do and some do not. Usually authors come to Abbeville because they have seen Abbeville books in bookstores and have admired them and decided that would be the right publisher for their project.

□ **Tell me about a book that was successful because the subject and timing were right.**
We recently published a book called *Cats at Work,* by Rhonda Gray and Stephen T. Robinson. We happened to be looking at various proposals for books about cats, but all were derivative. The next day I got a cold call from someone who said he'd like to submit a proposal about cats at work. I said, "Come right in"— that never happens. The young man came in with his proposal. He had a fresh idea as well as superb pictures of cats in various workplaces. Almost immediately we decided to do the book. We published it within six months. We've now got a postcard book and plans to do note cards. I don't think the author has any idea how unusual it was that this all came about so quickly. So there are some good things that happen, if the subject is right and the timing is right.

□ **What if someone comes in with only one skill—a photographer without text or a writer, or an author without photographs or a photographer?**
That's a very good question. That's exactly what happened with a book we published on Provence. The photographers were photographer's photographers. Their pictures of Provence looked like paintings. They had been coming in for a few years, but they just didn't know what to do with their pictures. I believed in them. I really thought the pictures were fantastic. But I couldn't convince anyone in the marketing department that this was a book. I enlisted the help of our editor in Paris to find an author to write a text. The text is almost as interesting in its way as the photographs. I worked with the photographers to group their pictures into themes, because they really didn't know what to do with them. And the book has just been published. I'm really very pleased.

□ **This book on Provence is really your creation.**
With illustrated books, that's what happens. Many of the ideas are created in-house or in collaboration with authors or photographers. That happens all the time.

□ **Do you have words to the wise for authors in search of a publisher of art or illustrated books?**
Timing and luck play a tremendous role in getting a book published. Assuming that one has timing and luck, I think an author should be prepared to take advantage of any opportunity with a well-conceived and well-written proposal. Once the book is accepted, the author should do everything necessary to do the best book possible—which is the same goal as the publisher's.

If the writer believes in the project, he or she should pursue it. The reasons for its rejection by a publisher may have nothing to do with its merit. The rejection could stem from a publisher's current program—there may be a competing book already on the list, or the marketing department may be convinced that they can't sell enough copies of the book to make the cost of producing it worthwhile.

A writer should try another house and remain positive. If the proposal is superior and the timing is right, I believe the book will be published.

23

Books as Artifacts

NION McEVOY, EDITOR IN CHIEF AND
ASSOCIATE PUBLISHER
Chronicle Books
San Francisco

NION McEVOY, Editor in Chief of Chronicle Books, was an attorney at
the William Morris agency in Beverly Hills before he joined Chronicle
Books in 1986 as acquisitions editor. McEvoy rose from acquisitions editor
to executive editor, and became editor in chief in 1991. He is presently in
charge of Chronicle's acquisitions process and editorial department.

Founded in 1968, Chronicle Books produces inexpensive, illustrated
trade paperback books. The list includes James McNair's cookbook series
and Nick Bantock's best-sellers, *Griffin & Sabine, Sabine's Notebook,* and
The Golden Mean. Chronicle publishes approximately 209 titles per year
(125 adult, 28 children's, 56 gift works), including calendars.

☐ **You say that your books are artifacts. Please elaborate.**
Most of us grew up thinking about books as vehicles for literature or stories or
information, but what we're also very concerned about here is the art of the
book—the book as an object. What will continue to distinguish the book from
electronic competition is that the book, in and of itself, is an attractive object. It
has sensuous properties that are very appealing—the heft and feel of the paper,
the design of the book, which we take very, very seriously.

☐ **How would you define the books you publish?**
Books that are elegant, but affordable. I like to think that we publish for people
who have more taste than money. We do books that are beautifully designed,
beautifully printed, and yet not out of the price range of most customers.

One of the things that distinguishes us is that other art book publishers, like Abbeville and Abrams, tend to do the traditional, coffee-table book—higher priced, thicker, more serious. Ours are lighter, younger, livelier.

□ **How do you decide whether a book fits in your publishing program?**
It's a combination of things. We tend to make decisions in a fairly collegial way. There are things that I might respond to. I'm a drummer and I love rock music. I might tend to respond more enthusiastically to something like that. I rely on my colleagues to return me to a sense of reality.

There are certain questions that we always ask, even if a work is clearly publishable:

1. Is there an editor who really loves it or cares about the project so he'd be willing to put in the work necessary to make a good book?
2. Is there a market for the book? Is there an ascertainable group of people who would want this thing out there?
3. Can we produce it at a price that group of people will feel good about spending for the book?

□ **How long does it take to make these decisions—from receipt of a viable proposal or manuscript to the decision?**
Anywhere from briskly to too long, which is in reality the way it tends to work out. We have editorial board meetings every other week. Usually it takes a minimum of two to three weeks, depending on whether we have to do more research on it—to figure what's out there in the market, if there are production questions to be resolved, pricing issues (when you're doing visual books, you have to do color separations, you have to buy printing in Asia for the most part), and other production issues.

□ **How do your advances compare to other publishers'?**
They're competitive. They have to be or we wouldn't be in business. We've made offers of anywhere from $2,500 to $250,000.

□ **What are your royalties?**
Royalties for art or illustrated books are lower than for standard trade books because the cost of production is higher. Royalties for standard paperback trade books range from 7 percent to 10 percent, based on the retail price of the book.

□ **How do you find your books?**
Any way we can. Some come in through agents, some from authors, some we find at the Frankfurt Book Fair, where we buy North American or English rights from French, German, Japanese, or U.K. publishers.

Sometimes we have ideas ourselves. Often it will be a food book or something like that. We've worked with and know a lot of people in that community. It's not hard to find someone to do it. Sometimes we'll find a group of photographs we want to publish and we'll sit and think, "Who is the right author for this?"

□ **What are the chances of a first-time author getting published?**
They're not bad. The thing about visual books is that somebody doesn't have to sit and read through thirty, fifty, or one hundred pages to see whether it's publishable or not. You can look at the illustrations and transparencies and get a fairly quick feel for it. So even if it comes over the transom, usually you can get a sense of whether the subject matter is of interest and you get the illustration. Fiction really has to live in and of itself.

□ **How does an author's proposal for your books differ from that for a traditional nonfiction book?**
In some ways they should accomplish the same end. I tell people they should make a proposal as if they were talking to people with no imagination whatsoever. In other words, there should be enough material that there is no question about what each party envisions when they are contemplating the book. If it's an illustrated book, we have to see enough illustrations to envision the final book enough so that we can have a substantive conversation.

□ **Who is responsible for the artwork and design of the books?**
The author is responsible for the artwork, but not the design usually, unless the author is a designer.

□ **What in a proposal turns you on?**
Something that looks new or fresh. Perhaps it opens up a world that I was unfamiliar with before that I suddenly realize is fascinating and this is the way to enter it, to understand it.

Something that's witty and whimsical and fun and makes people laugh. Something that seems extremely useful and practical. Something that's beautiful. Anything that's valuable in one of those ways.

□ **What do you advise an author in search of a publisher?**
It's always better if the person knows something about the house that he or she is sending the material to. You go to the bookstore. In looking at who publishes what, and what current formats are out there, especially for an illustrated book, you want to be able to visualize the finished thing as fully as possible. You will have a much more realistic idea of what you can expect and you can also be much more focused. The more focused a proposal is on both what the house does and on how that book will fit into that house best, the better the finished book will be.

We're always looking for things that we don't expect. If we could expect everything, I, for one, probably wouldn't come in to work every day, because it would be too boring. It's difficult to say exactly what I want people to do. I want them to surprise me.

□ **Do you have any words to the wise for writers?**
Don't give up your day job. More seriously, consider collaborations with photographers and other artists. Remember the sensuousness of the object you seek to create.

24

Innovative Formats

GREG AARON, EXECUTIVE EDITOR
Running Press Book Publishers
Philadelphia

GREG AARON received a bachelor of arts degree in English literature. After graduation from college, he was hired as an assistant editor at Running Press. Three promotions later, he is now the executive editor.

Founded in 1972, Running Press is a privately owned trade house that publishes 150 books each year. Their general interest list includes children's books, hobbies, crafts, art, science, and classic fiction for children and adults.

Running Press receives about thirty proposals a week from a variety of sources. They accept unsolicited manuscripts, deal with agents, and receive proposals from book packagers. Sixty percent of submissions are received directly from authors; 40 percent are from agents. "We're always willing to work with first-time authors if they have a good idea," says Aaron.

☐ **Many of your books are in what might be called innovative formats. What are innovative formats?**
Innovative formats include books that range tremendously in their physical dimensions or are unique in other ways. For example, we create miniature books that measure 2³/₄ inches by 3¹/₄ inches. We've published books that fold out into wall charts that are 20 inches high by 8 feet long. Other interesting formats we employ include pop-up storybooks with narrated audiocassettes inserted into the back covers, and book packages that include books plus objects to use with those books. Over the last five to ten years, the definition of what a book is and what

bookstores are interested in selling have changed quite a bit. The definition of what a book is has been expanded.

□ **Please give me specific examples of book packages that you would not have seen in a bookstore five or ten years ago.**
We recently created a project called the *Make Your Own Book Kit*, which is intended for children six to twelve years of age. The kit includes a slipcase that contains a book about books—what books are, the history of book making, and instructions on writing and illustrating your own book—plus all the materials a child needs to assemble a book: thirty-two blank pages of paper, a needle and thread for sewing the pages together, two sets of endpapers, a blank preglued hardcover, a brush for glue, a dust jacket, and a book plate.

Another example is *Build Your Own Radio*, which contains a book about how a radio works, including all of the science and physics involved. The kit also includes the components that an eight- to twelve-year-old will need to build a working AM radio.

□ **Why are bookstores selling these innovative formats?**
They are different and eye-catching. They encourage creativity and hands-on learning and they make learning fun, which both parents and children love. The book is accompanied by an activity that you can't get anywhere else. You can't easily find the components to construct a hardcover book from scratch, for example.

□ **Tell me about the miniature books that you publish for children and adults.**
Our Miniature Editions are wildly successful. They contain a wide variety of material, including literature, art, and quote collections on friendship, love, and so on. They are sold in racks in the bookstores, so they're all displayed together.

Miniature books are difficult to create. Because of the space limitations, it requires a lot of planning and effort to develop the manuscripts and artwork.

The Miniature Editions are very attractive objects, small enough to fit into a pocket or the palm of your hand. People say they're not only fun to look at and read, but they're cute and make great gifts.

□ **What should authors include in a proposal for a book with an innovative format?**
I want to find out, first and foremost, the unique concept of the book. I want to understand what the project will accomplish and what the reader will learn from it. Usually, I don't have to see a full manuscript or sample spreads with art in

place in order to make a preliminary decision. If we have further interest, we may request additional materials.

If an author has an interesting idea and has demonstrated the ability to execute it, we'll structure a deal.

□ How are proposals for innovative formats different from those for other books?

The creation of a book in an innovative format requires a collaborative effort between the author and the publisher. The author knows what the book is going to be about. But if it's a kit, our production staff will probably design the package. We have to find the materials that are going into the kit, and then price and purchase them. We figure out the retail price and make sure that everybody is making some money. We have to juggle all the parameters to make sure that everything works.

□ How should a writer submit a proposal for a kit?

The author should give us an idea of what he or she sees in the book, including a table of contents, what will accompany the book, and a description of how it might work. The writer should not be attached to one particular size or execution because it may not be technically or economically feasible. We start with general ideas and parameters and then determine what works best.

□ Is the author responsible for illustrations when a book is art-intensive?

With most of our books, the author takes care of the text and we arrange for the illustration.

□ These books are obviously expensive to produce. How does that affect the amount of money that the author will earn?

When an author comes to us with a concept, we pay standard industry royalties of 6 percent to 8 percent, based on the book's retail price. Before we undertake any project, we do a basic profit and loss analysis in order to decide whether we can make a minimally acceptable profit. As the publisher, we're buying a project and assuming a large, calculated financial risk. We make sure it's going to work for us and for the author as well.

□ Do you offer advances?

The amount depends on the project, on the number of copies we think we can sell during a given time period, and the retail price of the project.

□ Have you ever given five- or six-figure advances?

Yes.

□ **Do you and your editors come up with ideas and find authors?**
Yes. Editors track trends and the tastes of the reading public, so we can some-times spot opportunities. When we come up with an idea, we'll seek out some-one with the expertise needed to write the book.

□ **How do you pay those writers?**
Sometimes on a flat fee basis.

□ **Are innovative format books satisfying to create?**
It's a very gratifying process, a labor of love for an author and the publishing staff. When a project is finally printed, appears in stores, and you get to hold a copy in your hand, there's a sense of accomplishment. You've created something that's different from anything that's ever come before it.

□ **What changes are you seeing in innovative formats?**
I'm starting to see books packaged with CDs and CD-ROM disks. We're seeing some very elaborate paper engineering projects, such as *The Art Pack* from Knopf, a package designed by Ron Van der Meer, a professional paper engineer. *The Art Pack* is an exploration of the principles of art, including perspective, color mixing, and so forth. The package contains an incredible array of techni-cal devices, including pop-ups, which enhance the reading process. As time goes on, there will be many more opportunities for authors to stretch the boundaries of what a book can be and publishers will continue to look for things such as this.

□ **Do you have advice for authors seeking a publisher of innovative formats?**
An author should know the publisher that he or she is submitting a proposal to. Go to bookstores, look at the books that the publisher is currently doing, and obtain a copy of their catalog. Many authors don't spend enough time research-ing before they choose publishers. We receive proposals for original fiction and poetry all the time, but we've never published that kind of material and probably never will.

Call the publisher and obtain the name of someone specific to whom you can address your proposal. That way it will be evaluated by the person who has the ability to understand it and eventually buy it.

Many authors (and even some agents) don't put enough thought into their proposals. For example, I regularly receive proposals with grammatical and spell-ing errors. Such lack of attention does not make me inclined to consider an author's work.

Make sure that your proposal is intelligently and gracefully presented. Create your proposal as carefully as you would a résumé. Don't waste time in getting to the point. Show us something unique, something that nobody has seen before. Or show us an old idea executed in a new way.

Be prepared to work in a collaboration. The idea is yours and the expertise is yours, and editors want to rely on an author's judgment. At the same time, we're all working together on a very complex project.

An editor is an author's business contact, his or her guide through the publishing process, and the person who can help a writer create the best possible manuscript. And a good book is something that can make everyone—author, editor, and reader—very happy.

25

Specialty Travel Books

JENNIFER BASYE SANDER, SENIOR EDITOR

Lifestyles Division
Prima Publishing
Rocklin, California

JENNIFER BASYE SANDER initially worked in magazine publishing and book retailing. Her job as a book buyer taught her how to choose topics that sell. As Sander listened to thousands of sales presentations, she frequently thought to herself, "Who do they think is going to buy this?"—a question she now asks herself when evaluating books. She is presently senior editor with the general books division of Prima Publishing.

Prima Publishing, founded in 1984, publishes approximately one hundred books annually in the general trade division and seventy-five books in the computer and computer game divisions.

Sander classifies her guidebooks as niche travel books. "We can certainly say what they're not," explains Sander. "They are not general guidebooks to a particular area. They are, rather, travel books geared to people with particular interests, going to a popular destination. Sort of a subgroup of tourists. It's not everybody going to Asia. It's more like, 'a food lover's guide to Asia.'"

☐ **How do you acquire your books?**
Between 5 percent and 10 percent are unsolicited queries. I'm happy to work with unagented and first-time authors—we publish about four per season.

The rest are divided among authors we've already worked with. What we really want are people we can work with over and over again. I don't have the time or the energy every season to come up with thirty-five new authors to write books for me.

With every list, there are probably two to three ideas that we have generated, that either I have thought of or the publisher has thought of, and that we're going out and getting people to write for us. Sometimes it's work for hire and sometimes it's saying, "Hey, we think this would work, why don't you write it?" For example, some years ago I was looking at *Publishers Weekly*'s best-seller lists. In the domestic travel best-sellers, four of the ten were books about the Southwest. And I was thinking to myself, "What can I do here? How can I carve out a piece of the action for myself?"

And then I remembered a writer of ours, Dave DeWitt, editor of *Chili Pepper Magazine*, who lives in Albuquerque, New Mexico, and writes all kinds of hot and spicy cookbooks for us. "I wonder," I thought to myself, "if he could do a food lover's handbook to the Southwest?" I called him up and he said, "My God, why didn't I think of it before? Of course I could do this book."

He wrote the book and we published it.

□ What do you look for in a really good proposal for a travel book?

I want a proposal that was done along professional standards. Someone who has taken the time to look at one of the books on how to write a proposal. It should include a nice letter that talks about what the overall purpose of the book is, a proposed table of contents, a proposed chapter outline, possibly a sample chapter or two.

It should give the author's idea of the size of the market and back that up. Don't just say, "Seven million people travel each year to Jacksonville, Wyoming." I want to know who said that. When I talk to authors on the phone, I say, "Put yourself in the frame of mind of somebody who is going to a bank to get a bank loan to start a new business. The kinds of things you would have to tell a bank loan officer in order to convince them that your idea is good enough to back with money." Because that's what a publisher is doing. We're backing your idea with money. We're publishing your book at great expense. So we need to know this information.

□ How does a proposal for a travel book differ from those for other nonfiction books?

Authors have to convince me that people are really and truly going there. I would be willing to take a flyer on a cookbook idea. With a food, business, or parenting book, I could probably decide on my own.

But with travel books, you need to publish a book that people are going into a bookstore to find, after they have already decided to go to a particular place.

□ How can an author determine travel trends?

By contacting the various tourism departments of particular countries, or collecting articles that talk about, for example, "the New Travel Trend to Costa Rica or Southeast Asia."

I know a lot about travel, but I'm sure there are movements within travel that I am not currently aware of. And I would need to be convinced—yes, people are going here and people are going to need this kind of book.

□ Does a travel writer need credentials or previous writing experience?

Not necessarily. I would probably be more interested if they had a lot of personal experience as travelers. But I'm willing to take a chance on somebody, if his or her writing is strong enough. When I first came to Prima, I received a letter from a woman who didn't have much in terms of travel writing credentials. She had a humorous column for *Working Mother Magazine* about being a mom with kids. She wanted to write a book about traveling to Walt Disney World with small kids, because she lives in North Carolina and went down there all the time and really felt that the market needed this.

I took it to the publisher during a meeting and said, "I think this book would work. There's this huge audience that goes to Disney World and many of them are traveling with kids. It's a huge quantity of the market. What we would be doing, essentially, is taking a very large market and chipping off our own small piece of it, creating our own niche." He said, "That's great! Why don't you show it to the St. Martin's rep in Florida" (because Prima is distributed by St. Martin's). The Florida rep said, "Yes."

Over and over and over again I had to prove to the publisher that yes, this is an idea that's going to work. So finally we published it and we sell fifty thousand copies a year. It's a fine little book.

This is a woman who, at first look, did not have the credentials to write this book, other than the fact that she lived near Disney World and her kids liked to go there.

□ How long does it usually take for you to make a decision on a proposal?

That's very, very slow. It's certainly two months. If I don't like something, it goes back right away. But if I'm interested, it's a pretty slow process. It has to do more with the publisher's schedule and how often we're able to get together for editorial acquisitions meetings. I wish it were faster.

□ Do you have pet peeves about writers?

Yes. I can't stand it when my name is misspelled. It sounds like a really petty thing, but beyond it being a petty little personal thing, it shows me that somebody isn't really taking the time. If they didn't take the time to make sure they got the name right, that shows me a sloppy attitude and a rush job and that things will never get better.

I also have a real bias against people using old typewriters. It's sad to say, but the minute I open up a proposal and I see that it was written on an old typewriter, I think—and, invariably, it has turned out to be true—"This is somebody who hasn't written anything in the last twenty years and is sending me a lot of clippings from stuff that they've done in the 1950s and 1960s; they just want to get back into writing, and aren't up to date with current methods." It also says to me that this person isn't computerized and that's going to cost a lot more in production. My contracts call for two copies of the manuscript and two copies of the disks.

It's a sad thing because typewriters are wonderful old things. It just shows me that they're not in tune with what's happening today. I think people need to be.

Again, it all goes back to the fact you are literally trying to convince a bank board to loan you money. Obviously, it's not a loan. If people would put themselves in that same frame of mind, that essentially a book is like a small business and somebody else is backing them to do it. It's all about money. At least nonfiction publishing. I'm sorry to say it's not about literary worth, it's not about the beauty of words. It's about money. It's about whether we should take a gamble on publishing your book.

☐ What kind of advances do you offer?

We offer sane advances. The smallest amount I would offer is about $2,500. I have paid five figures and offered six figures.

I do pay sane advances because we like people to be immediately in the black, up and running earning royalties from the first royalty period out. I'm not going to pay somebody a whole bunch of money thinking, "Well, we're never going to earn this back and that's all this guy's ever going to see." We look for books with serious backlist potential, books that can be on the shelves for years and years and years. We're not interested in something that has a short shelf life. We want something that's going to be around for a long, long time and hopefully, both the author and the publisher are going to make a lot of money.

☐ Can a travel writer expect to receive media coverage for his or her book?

We try to get reviews in the appropriate magazines, and if it's the kind of thing that radio people are interested in, we try to book radio interviews. I'm not going to get a travel writer on "Oprah."

☐ Do you have words to the wise for authors in search of a publisher?

Keep trying, but be honest with yourself about your book's potential and salability. If you can't find a publisher and you think you have a really great idea, publish it yourself. There's no reason why you can't make something work.

□ **Does self-publishing work? Can self-published authors distribute their books to the chain bookstores and independent bookstores? Can they receive reviews and publicity?**

It's a pretty easy thing these days, with more and more people being computerized. Getting it to the wholesaler and getting the word out through creating your own publicity, and having people go into bookstores and asking about your book. The bookstore's going to pick up the phone and call the wholesaler. There are a lot of books on the market that can tell you how to do that.

I'm all in favor of people getting away from the mystique of being published by somebody else. And this is another element that they should use while trying to decide the same business about appearing before a bank board. Would they put their own money into doing something like this? Because if they wouldn't, why are they asking somebody else to? If you think, "Now this would never work as a self-published edition," what makes you think it's going to work if Random House publishes it?

I'm always very impressed and pay great attention when somebody says, "I self-published this and just in my own city I was able to sell two thousand copies."

26

Self-Help Books

TONI BURBANK, VICE PRESIDENT
AND EXECUTIVE EDITOR

Bantam Books
Division of Bantam Doubleday Dell Publishing Group
New York

TONI BURBANK, Vice President and Executive Editor of Bantam Books, was an English and French major in college and did graduate work in English. After graduate school, she worked at Columbia University Press for one year. In 1967 she went to Bantam as an assistant editor in the school and college department. She has long since moved to general trade. Burbank edits nonfiction. Her list includes maternity and child care, women's interest, and psychology and health books, with a particular emphasis on mental health.

Bantam Books, a division of Bantam, Doubleday, Dell, publishes more than twelve self-help books each year out of hundreds of proposals. Founded in 1945 as a mass market paperback publisher, Bantam today publishes general interest books in all formats.

□ **Do you publish books by first-time authors?**
Yes. One of my great pleasures is working with first-time authors. I enjoy walking people through their first publishing venture. It's very exciting. People's lives change when they write a book. I love being part of that.

□ **How do their lives change?**
When they are professionals, as many of the senior authors of self-help books are, publishing a book means a quantum leap in terms of reputation and prac-

tice. These well-established professionals are not compensated for writing the book at the income level to which they're accustomed, but the repercussions for their reputation and overall practice are huge. They become one of a handful of professionals who have been published.

I think that there's something transforming about putting the truth that you stake your life on into book form. It's a wonderful coming out in the world.

□ How can a freelance writer, who has no credentials, publish a self-help book?

The top freelance writers team up with people who have professional credentials. I can't imagine publishing a book by someone who has simply studied up on a topic. No matter how good he is, we would suggest that he get a senior person to work with.

□ Are there exceptions?

There are always exceptions to prove the rule, whether it's Gail Sheehy, with *Passages,* or Colette Dowling, who recently published *You Mean I Don't Have to Feel This Way?* Sheehy and Dowling bring best-selling author credentials to a topic. They were extremely seasoned writers when they approached their first self-help books.

□ How do you acquire most of your books?

Most of them are agented but I have bought books from authors over the transom.

□ What should a complete self-help book proposal include?

A very clear statement of the book's mission, an outline, a couple of sample chapters, and a review of competitive works in the field. And, of course, the author's credentials.

□ What makes a winning proposal stand out from a loser?

A simple answer is that it's new—a topic we don't have. Or a topic that has been popular on other lists but with a new approach. It must be well written with a solid outline. The author should be well known in the field. It's not just one thing, but the way the entire proposal is presented. We know almost from the first page whether authors are on top of their topic.

□ How does a self-help proposal differ from a nonfiction proposal?

The key to a self-help book is a targeted audience—people with a certain problem that they need to solve. The success of a self-help book depends on how the audience is addressed and the kind of voice that the author has toward that audience. The pace must be right, the tone of voice toward the reader must read true, and the information must be presented in a way that the reader can easily identify with.

I want to see at the proposal stage that the senior author is on a lecture circuit—that he or she does presentations, workshops, that kind of thing. We find it extremely helpful for an author to be "out there."

□ **Do you ever withhold an offer if the author isn't presentable or articulate?**

Yes, indeed. Pretty or handsome is not the issue. Articulate and compelling is. We've received proposals that were worth pursuing to the point that we invited the author to talk with us. Then we discovered that the person could not present the material effectively. If we can't see the author in person, we'll speak at length on the telephone. We can tell a lot by that. Again, we're not looking for personal beauty. We're looking for the alacrity of response and how interesting the person is.

□ **Do all self-help books require a spokesperson?**

Some books don't necessarily need a spokesperson.

□ **How do writers promote their self-help books?**

We usually plan author appearances. We try for national shows. Full-scale national tours are less frequent because in the last ten years, local daily talk shows have become fewer in number. We often arrange appearances in a town where the author is going to be.

□ **What range of advances do you offer writers of self-help books?**

It's extremely wide. If it's a hot topic and the writer is agented and the book is auctioned, the numbers can go very high, over six figures.

□ **How does the editor-author relationship work?**

The most important thing is that authors see it as a working partnership with me. We both have a tremendous vested interest in this book and a tremendous commitment to it. They can call on me and I can call on them to do the best possible job we can together.

I usually work very early with an author on the outline. I almost always invite authors to tell me how they'd like to work, what's best for them. Some people like to go away and write the whole book without sending a piece of it. I usually urge them to send me a couple of chapters early. If there are any obvious problems, we can solve them before they get too deeply into the book. Some people want to send in every chapter as it is completed.

□ **How do you verify that the work is accurate, good, and sound?**

We assure that the book is good and sound through the author's credentials. That, in effect, is our best assurance: that we're getting someone from the top of his or her profession, who already has a good reputation and will be writing a book in line with that. We don't have a formal review system.

We send books to people for endorsement quotes. Occasionally, a question will come up from those readers.

We also have in-house people with a great deal of informal but real expertise in these areas. There are certain books to which I bring quite a bit of lay knowledge. That's one of the supports that I can offer to authors.

□ Do you have advice for authors in search of a publisher?

Be well prepared. First impressions count. On more than one occasion, I've had someone send me a proposal who, two weeks later, tells me, "That was really a draft, here's the real thing." Or, "Let me send you some supplemental material. That really wasn't enough." The first impression is very hard to dissipate once it has been made.

An enormous amount of attention should go to the proposal. We editors always say among ourselves, "If this person can't write a good proposal, what is he or she going to do with the book?" You can't just throw together a proposal and say, "When it comes to the book, I'll really do it."

□ Do you have pet peeves?

I'm astounded when I get proposals that are full of typos. It sounds petty. But to me it's a symbol. This author is trying to sell the book. What kind of problems will I have when he's not trying to sell it anymore, when it's just the book and his friendly editor at the other end? How much will I be expected to fill in?

□ What turns you on?

What really turns me on is that the author has in some way been preparing all of his or her life to write this book. There is a tremendous commitment on the author's part to this work. That commitment will evoke a mirroring commitment in me. That's publishing at its best.

We often see writers who have struggled with a problem themselves. I recently edited a book in which the author said that her most valuable credential was one that she never would have sought out—she had to get over a phobia. She had professional credentials, but the real impulse behind her work was to help other people as she herself had been helped.

27

Books on the Outdoors

PETER BURFORD, VICE PRESIDENT
AND PUBLISHER
Lyons & Burford Publishers
New York

PETER BURFORD, Vice President and Publisher of Lyons & Burford, was an English major in college, worked at Crown Publishers as an editorial assistant after graduation, and moved up the ranks at Crown to associate editor. He then became editor at Nick Lyons Books, a packager of fishing books.

Founded by Nick Lyons in 1978, Nick Lyons Books was a wholly owned subsidiary of an English company. In 1984 Nick Lyons and Peter Burford decided to "unpackage themselves," bought back all of the rights to the packaged books that they sold to other publishers, and began publishing and distributing on their own. They changed the name of the company to Lyons & Burford in 1988.

Their list includes books on natural history, the literature of the outdoors, fishing, tennis, golf, camping, backpacking, and some gardening and cookbooks. They publish virtually no fiction.

Lyons & Burford receives four to five hundred proposals annually, and publishes approximately fifty. Burford and Lyons look at everything. "I don't necessarily *read* everything," Burford confesses.

☐ **What do you look for in a proposal for a book on the outdoors?**
I look for a sense that whatever the specialized subject might be, whether it's camping or outdoor cooking or bird watching, the author is next to or the very

best person who could possibly do it. He's someone who has really studied the subject and has some real credentials for it. The author doesn't necessarily need professional or academic credentials, but there must be a sense of dedication to this particular subject. I want a proposal that's really very well thought out, very professional, and very authoritative.

We did a book called *Birding for Beginners* not long ago. The author doesn't have academic credentials in biology. But I know her well. I know that she is very passionate about the subject and writes very well about it. I know that what she has to say is really good, solid, practical material.

□ How do you ascertain that the material is authoritative?

I look at who the author is and what he or she has already accomplished. Has he or she published other things in the field, either magazine articles or other books? If not, what is there in this proposal that tells me that this person really knows what he or she is talking about? That, to me, is paramount—that I can be confident that this material has real authority behind it.

A birding book, for example. I don't pretend to be an expert on birds, but there are a lot of people who are. Many of them own bookstores that cater to birders. Those people are going to know right away whether a book rings true or not. I have to make sure that it will.

□ Do you worry that you might make a mistake?

It's not that I feel paranoid that I may make a fool of myself by publishing the wrong book. Usually I can tell. It's really an editor's job, I guess, to be a dilettante and know a little bit about a lot of different things. You never know until you open the proposal what the subject of a book might be. It helps to have at least some little nugget of knowledge about it that can tell you as an editor and as a reader, "Yes, this looks like the genuine article." You also have to trust the author that all of the details are correct. But for an overriding sense of whether the proposal rings true, ultimately it's the editor's responsibility.

□ Do you ever pass the proposal on to someone who is an expert in the field?

Sometimes I do, if it's a subject area that's very technical or if I truly have no sense at all about whether it's valid. Or when there's someone who may know the field and the competing books better than I. By way of illustration, I received a proposal for a book on tennis for doubles play. I know that most people who play tennis play doubles, and I know that the author knows what he's talking about, but I passed it along to someone else to see if it's a book that's of practical value to the average player. Are there competing books that already cover this material? That's something that I could determine on my own with some digging, but it's simply more efficient to turn it over to someone who knows the field.

□ **What do you want included in a proposal?**

I'd like to see a table of contents, a sample chapter that comes from somewhere kind of midstream in the manuscript—not the introduction or chapter 1—something that will give me a good sense of what the meat of the book is going to be. Some sample illustrations, if illustrations are appropriate. And a one- or two-page treatment on what this book is, which can either be a separate sheet or inherent in the cover letter from the author. What this book is, why the author considers it important, what other books in the field might be, and why this book differs from them. It isn't necessary to go through a long marketing proposal for a book, particularly in specialized fields. I know there are a lot of tennis players, golfers, and fishermen in the world. It seems a little amateurish when an author writes to me that there are fifty million fishermen in the United States. They're not all going to buy this book, as much as the author might like this to happen.

□ **How long does it take you to make a decision on a proposal?**

Sometimes it's as little as one minute, if it's something that's just inappropriate. It can go as long as a month or two for a book I want to ponder seriously.

□ **How do you acquire most of your books?**

A third are proposals from authors or agents. A third I dream up on my own. And the rest come from existing authors.

□ **What happens when you dream up a book on your own? How does that work?**

I perceive a need for a book, either on our list or in the world at large. I then look for an author to do it. I read a lot of magazines, everything from *Backpacker Magazine* to *Natural History* to *Orion Nature Quarterly*. A lot of times I get ideas from them, either from an article someone has already written, which is probably the most common thing, or just something I read that sparks an idea.

For instance, I read a piece in *Outside* magazine called "This Dog Is Legend" about a fishing guide in Florida, who had a dog who would retrieve cinder blocks from fifteen feet of water. It was a marvelous piece—it was funny, beautifully paced, and well written. And it had a very powerful, emotional, and wistful ending.

I wrote to the author and suggested we collect and publish some of these essays in book form. We did, and the book, *Batfishing in the Rainforest*, did extremely well for us. It was sold to Quality Paperback Book Club. We sold paperback rights on it to Holt. It was reviewed by Christopher Lehman-Haupt of the *New York Times*.

□ Who is responsible for illustrations?

Generally, in our contract it's the author. That can vary a lot, depending on the deal we strike and the nature of the artwork.

□ What advances and royalties do you offer?

Advances can be as low as $1,500; $3,500 would be the upper range. We never give big advances. The royalties we give are competitive with those of everybody else—10 percent of retail on hardcover.

□ Do your authors get media coverage?

Yes, when it's appropriate. Certainly to a lesser extent than they do at larger houses. But sure. We recently did a book called *Indian Creek Chronicles*, for which the author did a reasonably extended tour of the Rocky Mountain states and the Pacific Northwest.

□ Would you turn down an author who wasn't telegenic or mediagenic?

No.

□ Do you have any pet peeves?

Yes. Proposals on continuous form paper, where the paper isn't cut. It drives me crazy. I seldom read more than the first page.

Being very picky about contracts annoys me. Not necessarily pickiness, but argumentativeness. It drives me nuts when authors either write or get on the phone and argue about how much money we're making as a publisher and how little the author is making. It's kind of a myopic view, without a sense of the risks we're taking and the really small profit margins that we're working with, especially with specialized books, which, by their very nature, are not going to sell in large numbers. We can do print runs as low as three thousand copies. It's very hard to make a significant profit on a sale like that. That may be the extent of the sale of the book, if it's a very specialized book. I'm still happy to do books like these, but it does drive me nuts when authors feel they can come on like Peter Benchley, and make me out to be the greediest guy in the world.

□ Do phone calls annoy you?

No. Phone calls don't annoy me. That's what I'm here for—to talk to authors.

□ Do you have words to the wise for authors in search of a publisher?

"To thine own self be true." By that I mean, frame your proposal for a book on your terms. Don't go casting around for why a particular subject is trendy or really hot right now. That tends to be a tip-off to an editor that it's probably had its day already, if everybody is perceiving these trends. It's much more important to be oneself, to represent the book honestly, and to say why *you* think it's important, not why the rest of the world will.

Environmental Books

JAMES COHEE, SENIOR EDITOR
Sierra Club Books
San Francisco

JAMES COHEE, Senior Editor, has had an unusual career. He majored in English literature, but taught mathematics in a junior high school after college. He traveled and took various odd jobs in the United States and Canada. In his thirties, he entered graduate school and worked part-time with the Sierra Club. Although he had no editorial experience, he began doing freelance work for them, reading proof and manuscripts. When the publisher of Sierra Club Books decided to enlarge the company in 1979, he hired Cohee as a permanent staff editor. Forty-nine-year-old James Cohee has never worked for another publisher and has been in his present position since 1988. His specialty is nonfiction, literature, travel books, and books about environmental issues.

The Sierra Club was established by John Muir and a group of Bay area professionals in 1892. Their aim was to protect California forests and particularly to protect forests that were threatened in what is now Yosemite National Park. The Sierra Club first published books about exploring California in 1901.

☐ **What is an environmental book?**
Environmental is broadly defined. The categories are very wide. We have published poetry, fiction, pictorial books, collections of scientific papers, and books on environmental issues, travel books, histories, and more.

☐ **Do other publishers produce environmental books?**
I think all of the major publishers do good environmental books.

□ **Do you publish any books that are not environmental?**
In one way or another they are all environmental books.

□ **How many proposals do you receive?**
I look at about five hundred a year. The program publishes thirty.

□ **Do you deal with agents?**
We do deal with agents. We're probably talking about 50–50, agented and nonagented authors. Ninety percent of the proposals I see are directly from writers and are not agented or represented in any way.

□ **How difficult is it for a first-time author to get published with Sierra Club Books?**
It's difficult. In light of the volume of material we receive and the small list that we have, we publish a very small percentage of those who want to be published here.

□ **What, specifically, do you look for in a proposal?**
The author who submits a succinctly phrased letter, a precis, a table of contents, and one chapter is going to get a response fairly quickly. Those are the four things that I would recommend. It makes the editor's work easier.

I want a cover letter that is short. It should not exceed two pages and should describe the project, not only in aim, but include any book production specifications that the editor will need to know about. This isn't terribly important if you're writing a novel, but it's essential if you are sending a proposal for an illustrated book to us. The cover letter should include the author's qualifications to write the book.

It's very helpful for the editor to get an understanding of what shape this book might take. I would encourage an author who is submitting a photographic proposal, for example, to make guesses at not only the trim size of the book, but the number of pages, the number of photographs, and the number of pieces of color and black and white in the book. One of the things an editor is responsible for is determining the cost of producing this book. All of the financial transactions that occur between the editor and the author depend, in good measure, on the expenses the publisher incurs to produce the book and the commercial life this book might have. Anything the author can do to clarify for the editor how expensive a book we're talking about is very helpful.

The second thing a book proposal should have is a precis. That is simply a boiled-down description of what the book is. We're really talking about the body of the book. What is it? Is it a collection of pieces or is it a long essay or is it a pictorial book with text? What's its subject? How wide-ranging is it, and how long is it?

The third requirement for the proposal is a table of contents. It's helpful to have it annotated, but it doesn't need to be. This is something an editor can use not only to brief himself on what the book is, but to distribute to colleagues. We frequently share proposals and pick each other's brains about values and problems of various proposals. Material that the aspiring author provides is very helpful because it's easy to share.

The fourth is a sample chapter. I frequently get complete manuscripts, and I'm willing to go at them. But it's probably easier for the writer to send one chapter.

□ **Why do you want a sample chapter rather than the entire manuscript?**
I can quickly tell if it's possible for us to do the book. That's the first question that I ask myself. If I see a chapter that I like, that seems appropriate for Sierra Club Books, and the book has enough commercial life to earn back its costs, it's easy to go to the phone and get the rest of the material.

A sample chapter enables the editor to get back to the author more quickly.

□ **How long does it usually take you to make a decision on a proposal?**
It depends. If it's something that we can't do, I decide very quickly. But it will take longer if I'm interested in the proposal. I'll need to share materials with my colleagues, particularly the marketing director and the publisher. It might go out for readings to Sierra Club activists or experts for their review.

□ **How long would that take?**
It may take two months. It may take less.

□ **Do you mind if the writer calls after a month to see what's happening?**
No. I don't mind. I can usually get back to everyone within a month.

□ **What range of advances is offered?**
At the low end they're $2,500. Our advances have gone up as high as $50,000.

□ **How are advances determined?**
Advances are not numbers that come out of an editor's head. With the precis and other information in hand, the editor asks the production people for estimates on the cost of printing the book at a certain print run and a certain size. With the coaching of the marketing director and the publisher, the editor will decide what a reasonable print run would be. From this and a guessed book price, we determine the author's royalties on the sale of all of the books from the first printing. I want to underline first printing. At this stage in the game, we're not

doing any pie-in-the-sky guesses about what the life of the book might be. We are looking at what happens if we sell out all of the books we print in the first run. The author's advance is a fraction of his or her earnings on that run.

□ What royalty do you give your authors?

If it's a trade book, it's usually 10 percent hardcover, 7.5 percent softcover, based on the list price. That will slide up for hardcover books.

For photographic books, the royalty is calculated on a net receipts system because the publisher's expenses in publishing these books are huge. I don't want to give you a ballpark figure there because it varies tremendously. Also, the royalties can vary on books that the publisher is intent on doing, but don't have much of a commercial life.

□ Why would you publish a book that does not have much financial potential?

We publish some books in the public interest—books that the club has a commitment to, books that are done to fight the good fight, but which all parties understand are not published with any dreamy hopes of a big commercial life.

□ Is Sierra Club Books a profit-making organization?

Sierra Club Books does make a contribution to overhead for the Sierra Club, a public interest organization that is not-for-profit.

□ Would you rule out a proposal, if the author has no qualifications?

It makes it difficult, but I wouldn't rule it out. Normally, if a person is writing an environmental book that covers a subject the club is politically engaged in, the manuscript is sent to an expert to be read. If the author is not qualified to be part of this argument, it's going to be difficult to see the manuscript through.

□ What do you do in terms of publicity for your authors?

We do a lot. We have a marketing and publicity staff. When a book is contracted, they introduce themselves to the new author and send a twelve-page questionnaire. They cooperatively do a lot of work to make sure the public knows this book is available when it is available. They will schedule tours, if there are tours, and book interviews, if there are interviews. They will plan and prepare advertising copy. Our books are marketed and sold by Random House. The publicity people will front the author to Random House's sales team of fifty-five reps that canvas the entire country, brief them on the book, and hook them into that sales effort.

□ **Do your authors receive major media coverage—TV morning programs and talk shows?**
Sierra Club authors have received that kind of coverage. We have been on "The Today Show" and "Phil Donahue."

□ **Do you have pet peeves about authors?**
I don't have many pet peeves. Most of the people I work with, including the novices, are nice, reasonable people. I'm not usually pestered by them.

□ **What are some clues to help authors get published?**
Don't send a proposal to a publishing house you don't know. I frequently get proposals for books that have nothing to do with the Sierra Club. It's clear that the person sending it to me doesn't know what I do and doesn't know anything about the club.

Never send a letter addressed "Dear Editor." You can always find the person's name that you're sending material to in the *Literary Market Place* (LMP), a directory of publishing houses in the United States, and it has names, phone numbers, and addresses. You can find it at your library or you can purchase it. I appreciate it when I open a letter and it is addressed to me personally and it comes from someone I've never met or heard of. I know they've done some homework.

Write or call a publishing house for a catalog. They're free. A catalog is very helpful because it shows you what the publisher is interested in, and it's a good early-warning system for writers who are sending their manuscripts to an inappropriate publisher.

□ **With editorial turnover, the names in LMP might be outdated. Do you think authors should call a publisher to get an editor's name?**
I would second the suggestion to call and get a name.

□ **Do you have other advice for writers?**
Educate yourself about publishing. Get the big picture. From the writer's vantage point, it is much more than closing that door and knocking out that book.

A professional attitude comes from some knowledge of how books are written, edited, produced, publicized, and sold. An author should understand what he or she is doing in the context of the industry that the manuscript is headed for. A writer who has any illustration in a book should know what a halftone is and how halftone cameras work. Photographers who work in color should inform themselves about the four-color process.

Begin a shelf of books not only about the craft of writing, but about the industry of publishing. When I started as an editor, I found a little book called *Pocket Pal*, a primer of lithography, which was tremendously helpful.

I get a lot of questions, requests, and sometimes moody conversations from writers who don't understand that a book team isn't just a writer and editor. It is a very large number of people. It may be well over fifty people.

It is helpful for a writer to understand what comes of the solitude of research-ing and writing a book. The manuscript goes into a world that is the intersection of ideas and commerce. It's this world of commerce that few writers really understand.

29

Religious Books

MARY CATHERINE DEAN, SENIOR EDITOR
GENERAL INTEREST BOOKS AND RESOURCES
Abingdon Press
Nashville, Tennessee

MARY CATHERINE DEAN began her publishing career at St. Martin's Press in New York. She went to Abingdon in Nashville in 1983, where she worked her way up from production editor to copy editor, to associate editor, to editor, and ultimately to her present position as senior editor in the general interest books and resources section of Abingdon Press.

Abingdon Press, started in 1789, is the trade publisher for the United Methodist Publishing House. The 100 to 125 titles published each year don't necessarily come from the 3,500 unsolicited proposals they receive. A significant number of books are solicited by editors. Abingdon publishes almost all nonfiction. According to Dean, the few fiction titles deal with "exceptional persons—that is, persons with handicaps."

☐ **What categories do you publish?**
My list includes ethics, social issues, marriage and family, some Bible and Bible study, inspiration, devotion, Christian living, Advent and Christmas, Lent and Easter, anthologies, activities and crafts, and biography.

☐ **How do you usually acquire books?**
We have a stable of repeat authors. We're in ongoing conversation with them about our needs and their interests and where we might mesh. We rarely receive a proposal from them that we don't ask for and don't discuss before it comes in.

☐ **What do you look for in a good proposal?**

The author's background, training, credentials, previous writing experience, and whether the author has a network in the market to which the book is directed.

We see how the book fits with our program and gauge our ability to market it to the appropriate audience. We look for a demonstrated awareness of the market on the part of the author—a sense that the author is in touch with the audience and that this is a book that fills a hole or answers questions that a sizable number of people are asking.

We look at the author's ability to communicate on paper and how knowledgeable the writer is about the competition for the book under consideration.

What really is appealing is a well-organized, well-thought-out proposal that's easy to follow and somewhat catchy. It has to be a grabber. It has to be direct and simple, and communicate what it wants to be as a book. We ask for an outline and one or two sample chapters.

☐ **How does that proposal differ from one that is not directed to a religious publisher?**

If it is going to have religious content, we want to know to what extent it is religious and how the religious content is treated. Otherwise, it doesn't differ from any other proposal.

☐ **Will you look at proposals that do not have a religious focus?**

In the general interest section we do. The general interest books do not have to be overtly religious. It's a judgment call. An example would be our parenting book called *1001 Things to Do with Your Kids.* Such a book might be a religious book or it might not be.

☐ **The books in your Dimensions for Living imprint are directed toward a general market, but are "overtly religious." What does that mean?**

They all use religious language, tie religion into life in some way or other, and are more concerned with Christian living. Most contain at least some scriptural quotations.

☐ **Do you work with first-time authors?**

Fewer than 5 percent of our publications are from first-time authors. We don't necessarily have anything against them. It's difficult to break into the market.

☐ **Do you ever publish books from slush?**

Rarely. Once in a million years.

□ Do you deal with agents?

I do, although only a couple of books a year. Most of the other editors don't.

I think a lot of agents don't work with religious publishers as a rule. A lot of religious publishers don't work with agents as a rule.

Some of the smaller religious publishing houses weren't originally built on a trade publishing model. We were. If those smaller companies started out publishing pastors or people who were writers on the side, they didn't have to deal with agents. They could work directly with the writer, and money wasn't a very big issue because writing wasn't the writer's primary means of support. In addition, religious publishers traditionally have published out of a sense of mission and have difficulty competing for big-name authors. Some people in religious publishing equate agents with big money and are therefore wary of agents in general.

□ Once you develop a successful author, how is the relationship maintained?

It's an ongoing conversation. It's difficult with an author that we're publishing for the first time. We sometimes hesitate to commit to the second book until we see how the first book does. Once authors do really well, we want to keep them; we want to know what they're interested in working on next, or if their interests meet what the market tells us we need. It works both ways.

□ How do you determine books that are needed?

Market research, surveying competition, and concept testing. With concept testing we do a prototype of a book and send it to a selected list of people to get a response on it.

We can also gauge market need to a certain extent by surveying the slush pile. We have a person who screens unsolicited material. It's a yardstick of what people are interested in, trends, and that kind of thing.

□ Do you offer advances?

Only by exception to first-time authors. Yes to repeat authors. Advances are generally very modest, in the $1,000 to $2,000 range.

□ What royalties do you give?

For the first-time author, we start at 7.5 percent on retail. With repeat authors we often go to 10 percent—most of those will graduate at some point beyond the anticipated first printing.

□ What is your average first printing?

Between four thousand and six thousand books.

□ **Do you have pet peeves about authors?**

One thing that writers still do—and I can't believe it—is use generic salutations. It's hard to get past that. "Editors" or "To Whom It May Concern." At worst, "Dear Sirs." We know that we are on page 1 of any reference book that has anything to do with publishing because of our name. We get a lot of submissions because of our alphabetical location in those books. The person still has enthusiasm, hasn't gotten any rejections yet, has stamps and money.

For the religious market, if a writer says anything like, "The Lord told me to write this book," that's a big "no, no" to me.

We don't like simultaneous submissions. They're pretty obvious. In this computer age, people will change the name and address, but down inside the letter they'll say, "I hope you'll find this book worthy of Westminster's list." I can understand why authors do simultaneous submissions. It's not uncommon for a writer to wait six months while a publisher considers a proposal. I appreciate authors who are up-front, who will say, "In the interest of time, one other publisher is looking at this." I just want them to extend the courtesy of letting us know if another publisher offers a contract.

Another pet peeve is people who call on the phone. Believe it or not, writers call and try to talk their way into coming in person to tell us about the proposal. My attitude is, If you can't communicate on paper, why are you trying to write a book? I evaluate you as a writer by your ability to communicate through the written word.

□ **Do you have a word to the wise for authors in search of a publisher?**

Do all the research you can to determine whether your proposal fits the publisher's list. We always direct people to the *Literary Market Place* (LMP). But an easier way is to go to a bookstore and see which publishers are publishing the kind of book you want to write. Look in the acknowledgments and see if you can find an editor's name. A publisher can go through a change at the top and completely redirect emphasis and concentration. A house can hire an editor or an editor can leave, and some area of specialty disappears. Doing your homework tells you who is publishing what you want to do and perhaps even which editor is interested in the kind of thing you're thinking about. Put all that together and you might find a friend or ally.

30

Cookbooks

SUSAN FRIEDLAND, SENIOR EDITOR

DIRECTOR OF COOKBOOK PUBLISHING

HarperCollins Publishers
New York

SUSAN FRIEDLAND was a history major in college. Her jobs in publishing include editor at Harcourt school division, senior editor at Prentice Hall Press, managing editor at Arbor House, and copy chief at Playboy Press. She has been senior editor at HarperCollins adult trade division since 1988. Her specialty is cookbooks.

HarperCollins trade division publishes about three hundred books a year, including fiction, nonfiction, and reference.

☐ **Are cookbook authors usually agented?**
Most are represented by agents.

☐ **What percent of your writers are not represented by agents?**
Between 5 percent and 10 percent.

☐ **How do nonagented cookbook writers break through?**
I know them. I know their work. I read the magazines. I read their proposals.

☐ **How do you usually acquire cookbooks?**
Two ways. Either I have a good idea and give it to somebody. Or somebody approaches me with a good idea.

☐ **If you have an idea, how do you get an author to take on the project?**
I will attempt to match somebody with my idea. I will either approach a non-agented author directly or I'll say to an agent, "Here's this idea. Who have you got who can write it?" Or I'll call an agent and request a specific author.

□ **Do you usually find authors who have already written cookbooks?**
Yes. An editor has to be up to date on who is writing, who's writing what, and how well they do it.

□ **Will you offer a contract to writers you don't know?**
Usually, I know a writer's work. If I'm unfamiliar with someone's work, I'll ask for an extensive proposal.

□ **What kind of credentials do cookbook authors need?**
They must have published something, have a cooking school, or have a reputation I know. They have to be able to write and/or have something to say. They should be passionate about their subject, as demonstrated by previous writing or by a personal visit.

□ **Which authors get a personal visit?**
I'll see somebody as a courtesy to an agent or other business acquaintance. Of course, I'm always eager to meet people whom we have under contract or who have written something interesting.

□ **Will you take phone calls from someone you've never heard of?**
Yes.

□ **Do you read slush?**
Somebody reads slush.

□ **Is everything read that you receive?**
Yes. My assistant reads every proposal first and then I read it.

□ **What should a good cookbook proposal include?**
It must include a very good outline of the book. It has to have a contents page, chapter organization, and a dozen or so recipes. I have to see how the person can write recipes and how she plans to organize the subject.

□ **How does that proposal differ from other nonfiction proposals?**
It doesn't differ. The subject is different, as biography is different from a history book. This job is not about cooking. This is a job about publishing. I'm not running a catering operation. I'm publishing books.

□ **How long does it take you to make a decision on a proposal?**
It could take a minute, a month, or six weeks.

□ **What is the range of advances you offer?**
I offer anything from $5,000 to six figures.

□ **Who does the layout and illustrations in your cookbooks?**
We commission designers and illustrators. They are usually freelancers.

□ **What in a cookbook proposal turns you on?**
It's all very quirky. I have to see something intelligent. It has to be a good idea, an intelligent proposal, something that hasn't been done before that I think should be done, that I'm made aware of by this proposal and this author. Again, the proposal should reveal the author's passion for the subject.

□ **Are certain cookbooks in today and out tomorrow?**
Like everything, they have their moment.

□ **How would someone find a good idea for a cookbook?**
They have to go to the bookstore and see what's around. They should discover a hole and try to fill it, though not a microscopic one.

□ **To try to find a niche that hasn't been filled by other cookbooks?**
That's right.

□ **What turns you off about some authors?**
I dislike authors who don't deliver, who don't do what they say they're going to do.

□ **Do you have advice to authors of cookbooks?**
Do not try to sell me a book that has the same subject as one that was published a month ago. Study Harper's list to get an idea of the type of books we do.

□ **What do authors need to know to get published?**
Authors have to be aware of what's going on in the market. They've got to have something to say, and they should, again and finally, feel passionate about their subject.

31

Humor

LINDA GRAY, EDITOR
Contemporary Books
Chicago

LINDA GRAY majored in business and marketing in college. After graduation, she worked as a buyer for Neiman Marcus in Dallas, where she dealt with Contemporary Specialty Services, a book distribution company owned by Contemporary Books. When Contemporary Specialty offered her a buying position, she accepted and returned to Chicago, her home base. She climbed the ranks to vice president. In 1987 the publisher of Contemporary Books offered her the opportunity to try her hand at editorial. "One of the advantages of my background is that I see things from a marketing standpoint," says Gray. Her specialties are cookbooks, popular culture, and humor.

Contemporary Books began in 1947. Today they publish eighty to one hundred adult nonfiction titles a year. Contemporary places a strong emphasis on backlist titles, and its major subject categories include sports instruction, cooking, parenting, humor, and popular culture. The company, which was acquired by the Tribune Company in 1994, is the largest trade publisher in the Midwest.

☐ **What do you look for in a book of humor?**
I look for a book that is going to have a waiting market. It helps to have a name author such as Dave Barry or Erma Bombeck, but a book can also be helped by having a nationally known brand name attached to it, such as *Entertainment Weekly* or *National Lampoon*. We publish some of Lampoon's books. Of course, the subject of the book must be something that's of interest to a lot of people.

Last, the timing of the book must be dead-on. That's tricky, because books are sometimes acquired years before their publication.

□ **How do you know when there is a market for a humor book?**
It's a subjective call. A couple years ago, Francis Coppola's upcoming film Bram Stoker's *Dracula* was getting an enormous amount of hype. Because of that and the popularity of Anne Rice's books, we felt strongly that vampires had a good shot of being the "flavor of the month" for at least one season. I got a manuscript called "How to Get a Date with a Vampire"—a tongue-in-cheek spoof on the sexiness of vampires, which the Coppola movie was also supposed to exploit. The manuscript-book was funny, the subject was hot, and the timing was great, so we did the book.

Another example of books that rely on timing is the Dan Quayle quiz books (which were not published by Contemporary).

□ **What makes a book funny?**
That's a tough question. What one person thinks is funny, another person may hate, may not understand, or may think is stupid. Given that, I'd say a book is funny if enough people *think* it's funny.

□ **What do you advise an author who wants to publish humor? Is there a formula?**
I don't think there is a formula but it's very important to define your market and write to that market. If a writer wants to be published, I'd say that's the first thing to do—determine who the audience is. You can have what you think is the best book in the world, but if you don't know whom it will appeal to, nobody's going to read it; it's going to be a tough sell.

□ **What do you want included in a proposal for a humor book?**
It depends on the book. For cartoon books and books that rely heavily on visuals or lists, I like to see most, if not all, of the manuscript. They tend to be relatively short books, so that's not a big problem. If it is strictly prose, I want a synopsis, an author's opinion of the market and marketability, the competition, a chapter outline, and a couple of sample chapters at minimum.

□ **Who is responsible for illustrations?**
If the book depends upon illustrations, like a cartoon book, the author is responsible. If the book doesn't rely on pictures but I feel strongly that a few illustrations would help, it's negotiable. I've done it both ways.

□ **How do you acquire most of your humor books?**
Some are submitted by agents, some by the authors themselves. I've also developed my own concepts and found authors to write for me.

□ **How do you come up with concepts for humor books?**

Usually by following fads or trends—in movies, politics, music, whatever—which I can capitalize on. Once I come up with a concept, I work with agents and/or authors to find somebody to work with me.

□ **Do you ever deal directly with authors who don't have agents?**

Yes. Based in Chicago, we're not physically close to most agents. We deal more directly with authors than other houses might.

□ **Is it difficult for a first-time author to break into humor publishing, especially an unagented writer?**

It depends on the book's concept and the strength of the author's writing. You've got to have a really strong concept. You've got to be able to write. Unless I'm trying to play on the author's name, I don't care if he's written one book, ten books, or no books, as long as his writing is strong and the book has a strong market.

□ **Do writers need credentials to write humor?**

No. It's not like writing a book on brain surgery. You can write it or you can't.

□ **What kind of money do humor writers earn?**

It varies. Some probably earn nothing. Then again, what is Dave Barry earning these days—$1 billion? Royalties generally follow standard percentages for any other type of book.

□ **How long do you take to make a decision on a book proposal?**

From two days to six weeks, depending on how much research I have to do to check out competition and marketability of the work. It also depends on whether the editorial board "gets it" or not. If they need convincing, it takes a bit longer.

□ **Do you have pet peeves about authors—things they do that are annoying?**

People who think they are funny writers, and they probably *are* funny writers, but can't come up with an idea and then expect me to do it for them.

Another pet peeve is a writer who says, "Maybe there really isn't a market for my book, but it's really funny, so you should give it a shot."

Another pet peeve is when writers I've rejected, ask me to spend another half-hour giving them names, addresses, and phone numbers of other publishers to contact.

□ **Do you have advice to writers of humor who are searching for a publisher?**

If one editor hates your book, that doesn't mean it's not good. Try another publisher. You could even try different editors at the *same* publisher because humor is incredibly subjective. What I think is stupid, somebody else may think is hysterical.

32

Computer Books

DEAN HOLMES, ACQUISITIONS DIRECTOR

Microsoft Press
Division of Microsoft Corporation
Redmond, Washington

DEAN HOLMES has worked in acquisitions at Microsoft Press since 1988. After graduating from college with a major in English, Holmes "stumbled into a job" as copy editor with a multivolume general purpose encyclopedia. He worked as an editor and writer for Funk and Wagnalls Encyclopedia and as editor and account executive at the Meriden-Stinehour Press in Vermont before joining Microsoft Press in 1986. He climbed the ranks from acquiring editor, to senior editor, to managing editor, to his present position as acquisitions director (since 1988).

Microsoft Press was started in 1983 as the tradebook publishing arm of Microsoft Corporation. The list includes books about desktop personal computers and desktop applications, ranging from the basics (what a computer is) to the advanced (specialized programming books for developers). The company publishes approximately sixty books a year, including revised editions of backlist titles. They receive about two hundred proposals a year.

☐ **What is the nature of computer books?**
Many computer books are based on specific software programs that are released in a new version every nine, twelve, or eighteen months. When the new version is released, we revise our book to keep it up to date with the new version. At any given time, probably half of our current publishing program is the revision of

existing books. In the vast majority of cases, the original authors continue to revise them. We have a healthy backlist.

□ How do you acquire new books?
We perceive a need or a market for a particular book or topic.

□ What percentage of your writers have agents?
A quarter to a third.

□ How many are first-time authors?
Only 20 percent. Because many of the books are revisions, we usually have the experienced authors in place. But we do encourage new authors and new ideas.

□ Are writers' qualifications important?
Almost all of our authors are in the computer industry, in one way or another. Programmers, consultants, or journalists usually write the user-oriented application level and programming books. Academics occasionally contribute to the list as well. Many of our writers have computer science backgrounds, but some are history or English majors who have become interested in computers. Computer writers put themselves in the position of being experts, telling less knowledgeable people something that they want to know.

□ Do authors with a technical background also need writing credentials?
It sure would help. A lot of people who write computer books start out by writing magazine articles. We've done books by at least a half-dozen people who are contributing editors to or regular columnists for PC Magazine, for example. There are a whole bunch of computer-oriented magazines from the low level to the high developer end. It's rare for someone who hasn't done any of that kind of writing to pop up and have much success writing a big computer book.

□ Is there a lot of work for writers of computer books?
It's a big field. There's a large audience and a lot of work.

When I first got into computer publishing, I thought of it as a narrow niche. But if you go into the computer books section of a well-stocked Barnes & Noble, you'll be overwhelmed by the quantity and variety of books. It's a significant category for most booksellers.

□ Would you publish fiction with computers as a background?
We would probably consider it. We haven't done anything like that. An author with whom I was working at one point started writing a novel set in the computer industry. We were kicking around the idea of publishing it. He never finished it, so we were never actually faced with the question of what we would do.

□ How well do computer books sell?

I used to think that "real" publishing was fiction. They say that the average first novel sells five thousand copies. We sell a lot more books than that. In fact, our average book sells more than the average book in a lot of categories. Once you get into the niche of computer book publishing, you see that it's actually a small entrance to a large cavern.

□ How much money do computer authors make?

We pay royalties based on net rather than the suggested retail price. Our royalty for domestic retail sales is 10 percent to 15 percent of net. Our advances are in the $10,000 to $20,000 range. It's not megastuff. It is very much our hope and intention that advances pay back. We like to have everyone focus more on the royalty than the advance.

The range of economic benefit that an author of computer books can get varies widely. If we sell 10,000 copies of a $20 book, the author gets $1.25 a book or $12,000, which would be pretty shabby pay. We expect the books we publish to sell 20,000 copies or more. We have authors who have grown legitimately wealthy writing books that sell many hundreds of thousands of copies. Anything that sells 100,000 copies in the computer world is a highly successful book.

□ How long can books last in your backlist, with the constant changes in computer technology?

That is one of the big things that makes the computer book business different. It's a major issue. Most of our books have a shelf life of one year. It can be as little as six months. Every now and again there is a book that's good for three or four years. Our expectation is that every year or year and a half, a book will be revised if it has done well and the product or technology it is based on has succeeded and is moving forward.

□ How do writers get information about new computer and software technologies before everyone else does?

Most of the people we deal with are in the computer business. They have a good sense of what's going on in terms of products and technology. There are several computer magazines that specialize in keeping up with when the next version of so and so is coming out and other breakthroughs.

□ Does the computer industry give writers new information before it is released to the general public?

Yes. We publish a lot of books that have to do with Microsoft software products. Other computer book publishers also publish those books because Microsoft products are really big. The authors that we and other publishers work with often get on a list for beta software, which is software in development. Those writers receive the preliminary software when it is more or less hammered together, but not done and polished. It is stable and full-featured enough for them to map out their books and begin to write.

□ Is it imperative to have a computer book released simultaneously with the compatible software?

Timeliness is next to godliness in the computer book business, particularly for books aimed at users of spreadsheets or word processors. It is very important to have those books going on the bookshelf coincident with the release of that version of the software.

□ Is that different from other types of publishing?

Yes. I go to the ABA convention and see fiction books that are essentially done. Advance copies are there, yet the publishers say, "We'll be publishing these books eight months from now." Or you hear stories of books that have taken three, four, or five years in the making. Compared to that relatively leisurely pace, we and all computer book publishers are speed demons. It can be two years from the time a computer book author starts writing to the time a book is on the shelves. It can also be as little as three or four months. The average is somewhere in between.

This puts a lot of pressure on everyone. Everyone in the system is pushing all the time to try to move things along as quickly, but also as responsibly, as possible. You have to publish books that are accurate. That is the constant battle. One strong requirement for authors working in the field is that they are reliable in terms of schedule, that they recognize these pressures, and that they are willing and able to put up with them.

□ What are the nuts and bolts of a good computer book proposal?

A proposal usually needs to be connected to a specific software program, a specific software language, or a specific technology.

It needs to be timely.

We want to see a proposal that is similar in many ways to other kinds of nonfiction publishing. We need an overall description of the book and who it's for—a good definition of the audience. We also want a good pitch on why this book is important. Why will people want the book? If there are competitive books, which there probably are, what will distinguish this book from those books? What makes it better or one that someone would buy in addition to the competition? The proposal should have a well-developed outline, not merely a list of chapter names, and a paragraph describing what's in the chapters. It's good to know what kind of writing schedule the author proposes.

☐ **Can an author be assured that his or her written proposal will be looked at—and looked at seriously?**
Yes.

☐ **Do you accept phone calls from writers?**
A phone call is okay if someone is just saying, "Hi. Let me introduce myself and get on your list if something comes up." That person should always send in a follow-up résumé. There have been cases where two years after I had a phone conversation, something comes up, I'm looking for someone, and I say, "Ah, I think that person would really be good for this."

But if someone wants to propose a specific book, more often than not, the result of the phone call is, "Put something on paper and send it to me." Some people have the idea that the most important part of the process is schmoozing, that it's really important that they speak to you at great length on the phone or they arrange to meet you and explain their idea in detail. That's not all that valuable. It's more valuable to put the time and effort in something that is clear, detailed, and persuasive on paper.

☐ **Some authors worry about publishers stealing ideas from their proposals.**
This is true of inexperienced authors. People often call rather than send you something because they're not really sure of what happens in terms of ownership or confidentiality if they send you a book proposal. They think that you may say, "Wow, this is a great idea," and then ask someone else to do it. But we just don't do that. If someone comes in with a good idea that really is their idea, we would do it with them or not do it. We would treat it very much as their intellectual property.

☐ **Do you have advice for qualified writers in search of a computer publisher?**
Gather information about appropriate publishers. Get a copy of their catalog. What kind of books do they publish and what do they already have?

Find out from the publisher what information they want in a proposal. We have a little two-page document of thought-provoking guidelines to help authors put together a proposal. Often, when people make a cold call, we'll send them the guidelines.

Come up with a good idea that's not generic—something that may take a specific piece of software from a different, less mainstream angle. It may not necessarily be based on a piece of software, but is in the realm of computer business and is an original idea.

Get it down on paper. One great advantage of getting something down on paper that speaks for itself is that I can show it to the people I work with. When I talk to someone on the phone and he fills me with enthusiasm, there's no place for me to go with that.

33

Reference Books

CAROLINE SUTTON, SENIOR EDITOR

Facts On File, Inc.
New York

CAROLINE SUTTON has been senior editor in the adult reference division at Facts On File (since 1992). She majored in comparative literature in college. After graduation, she worked as an assistant at the William Morris agency in New York. She moved to Ticknor & Fields, a subsidiary of Houghton Mifflin, for six years, where she climbed the ranks from editorial assistant to associate editor before attaining her present position.

Facts On File, founded in 1941, was originally operated as a news service. The book division is ten years old. It is owned by InfoBase Holdings. Facts On File publishes 150 books each year—half are sold to libraries and half are marketed to the trade audience. All books are hard-core information reference. Facts On File publishes no fiction. "We don't do personal narrative nonfiction," adds Sutton. "We do some narrative nonfiction, but it must be very balanced, as objective as possible, and not polemic in any way."

☐ **What is a reference book?**
A reference book is any book that provides solid information about something in an objective and accessible manner.

A lot of our books are like encyclopedias, A to Z's. But the A to Z's can be anything A to Z. We have a Shakespeare A to Z, in which the entries are anything you ever wanted to know about Shakespeare but probably never wanted to ask—his life, his plays, the characters, Shakespearean critics, the sources of the plays. We also have a women's health A to Z, which functions similarly—everything you always wanted to know about women's health. We publish an encyclopedia of the Renaissance. You can organize almost anything in an A to Z format. It makes the information very accessible. It's an extra-easy way to do reference books. The material in a reference book must be balanced. It can be difficult to write a narrative and maintain that kind of balance. If you chop things up into an A to Z format, the balance almost imposes itself.

Our other books are organized chronologically or they are narrative. I recently edited a book on the wives of all the kings of England that was divided chronologically into chapters. There was a chapter about each queen. It was a very lively narrative. The librarians were crazy about it.

□ **How do reference books differ from educational books?**
Educational books are more like textbooks. We don't sell our books that way. We sell to individual school libraries, college libraries, and public libraries across the country. You probably could turn some of our high school oriented books into textbooks, but they're not set up to guide you through a course. They're really for someone who is looking something up.

□ **How do you usually acquire books?**
I acquire most of my books through agents because my background is in trade publishing. I know a scad of agents. But many reference editors acquire straight from the authors. Ninety percent of my list comes through agents.

□ **Why do so many of your authors come from the academic community?**
A good number are academics. The academic world, I've discovered, is a whole network beyond publishing. Many times I'll be looking for an academic. An agent will not find me one, but another academic will. Reference books are often more academically oriented. It requires, in many cases, a lot of expertise that someone with an academic background would have.

□ **Are credentials important for authors of reference books?**
Credentials are important, but they're more important for some books than others. For example, we signed up a book about the history of the American kitchen, which is written by someone who simply knows a great deal about the subject. On the other hand, I signed up a medical book about new treatments for varicose veins that's written by an M.D. That book would have to be written by an M.D. We sometimes hook a writer up with an expert. I have a legal book called *The Executor's Handbook,* written by a writer with a legal background and a lawyer.

Considering the depth that most of our books go into, you wouldn't be able to write one unless you had a really solid background.

□ **What distinguishes a proposal for a reference book from that for a trade book, and what do you look for in a proposal?**

One of the distinctive things about reference publishing is that you almost never see a full manuscript. Everything comes in as a proposal.

In evaluating a proposal, the first three questions I ask are: Is it a good idea? What are the author's credentials? What is the market?

If it's a good idea, is it useful? Does it hit a broad enough spectrum of the market? Would somebody really be interested? Does it fit in with things librarians are looking for now?

We also take a very close look at the competition. We have *Books in Print* on a CD-ROM and can search very quickly to find out whether, in fact, there are sixteen other books on any given subject. A trade publisher may be able to put a fancy spin on a book to make it sound terribly attractive to booksellers, even though a similar book has been done before. People aren't interested in the spin on a reference book. Whether it's a book buyer, a librarian, or a student, he wants the information that's in it. If the information is available elsewhere, no one's going to buy it.

And of course, we look at the writing, which shows up in the proposal.

□ **What makes a winning proposal stand out?**

It has a lot to do with the way it's reasoned. The writing has something to do with it. But, assuming that the book is good, and fills a need, and that the writer has credentials, the proposal must be clear, logical, and well-reasoned.

Reference books can't be whimsical. They can't be overwhelmingly personal. You can't just toss in your opinions, willy nilly. There's a lot to think about.

If you're doing an "A to Z," you always need to think about word count. The word count is very important because you must frame your project so it doesn't get completely out of hand. If you're writing an "A to Z," you don't start with A and end with Z. The first thing you do is compile a head word list, break it into categories, and assign word counts to each entry, based on how important the entry is.

□ **What information do you present to the acquisitions committee?**

When I've decided I want to buy a book, I make up an acquisitions packet, which includes the proposal, a word count, a trim size, a *Books in Print* search, an analysis of the competition, and a P & L (a profit and loss sheet, which tells the percentage of margin you're looking at), and, this is where we differ from a lot of other places—information from a library advisory board. We call librarians at various institutions all across the country with a proposal or an idea. We ask, "Do you like this, what do you think, do you have anything like it, does the price sound right to you?" We get their feedback. What they say is very important. I put all that information together, include my own memo, and take it to the committee. After we've talked about it, I turn down the proposal or I make an offer. We usually have acquisition meetings once every two weeks, but there are times when it lapses to once a month.

□ What kind of money do reference book writers earn?

We offer a 10 percent royalty based on the retail price of the book. The advances vary. It's not so much that they are lower than trade advances, but they often don't get above a certain level. In trade publishing, you'll see variations in advances—everything from $7,500 to $1 million. A hundred thousand dollars is a lot of money to pay for a standard reference book. Advances rarely go above five figures.

□ Do you get media coverage for your authors?

Yes. We have a certain amount of coverage in *Publishers Weekly*. We don't do a lot of book tours. Since our major market is the library market, sending an author on a book tour doesn't make the librarian buy the book. Librarians are completely unimpressed with that kind of thing.

□ Where are your books sold?

Libraries are our main market, but we also sell through bookstores and museum bookstores.

□ Do you have advice for authors looking for a publisher of reference books?

Make sure you are committed to the project. If you're going to take on a big reference book, make sure you're really committed because it's a large and unwieldy beast that you're going to have to live with for a long time. It takes an enormous amount of patience. Almost every first-time author I've worked with on a book that runs over two hundred thousand words has said, "I had no idea what I was getting myself into and how much work it involves." Some writers lose interest and don't finish their books.

If I were in trade publishing, I'd say get an agent. At a trade house, an agent can make a colossal difference. At a reference house, sometimes it will, but a lot of times it won't.

34

Textbooks

CLAIRE THOMPSON, SENIOR EDITOR
John Wiley & Sons, Inc.
Professional and Trade Division
Professional, Reference and Trade Group
New York

CLAIRE THOMPSON was an English major in college. After graduation, she landed a copy editing job at Harvard Law School. Four years later, she accepted a position at Allyn and Bacon, a college textbook publisher. "That was one of those wonderful 'learn-on-the-job' jobs," says Thompson. "We had a big bullpen full of young editors, each one responsible for the whole editing and production of ten new college textbooks, right down to the cover design." Thompson then went to Houghton Mifflin Company as assistant to the education editor. After her marriage, she moved to the New York area, where she worked as a developmental editor in the college division at Harper & Row (now HarperCollins). After seven years she joined Harcourt Brace Jovanovich (now Harcourt Brace) as a special projects editor. When HBJ's college division left New York in the early 1980s, Thompson moved down the street to Wiley. In 1987 she was promoted to editor for hospitality and tourism books, her present specialty.

John Wiley & Sons, founded in 1807, is the oldest independent publisher in North America. Wiley publishes about 1,500 books a year, and 30 percent of its publishing revenues comes from college textbook sales.

□ How do you acquire textbooks?

Textbook markets are clearly defined. A book must match the course that it will be used in. We look at the curricula of colleges and universities to learn what courses are offered, and then review the textbooks in use to discover where new books are needed. The largest markets are the basic courses: introductory psychology, principles of accounting, or beginning calculus, for example. Hundreds of thousands of students take these courses as freshmen or sophomores each year.

□ How do you decide that there is a need for a book?

If there aren't many books currently serving a course, there's an opportunity. Every publisher goes after the big courses, however. There are probably twenty-five introductory biology texts. The stakes are high, but so is the competition.

□ Is there a lot of competition in textbook publishing?

A successful textbook becomes very entrenched. In order to compete, some strategies are to find either a well-known author or someone affiliated with a well-regarded institution, to plan a more elaborately produced book, one that makes the instructor's job easier, and so forth. A new book should not be too drastically different from those currently in use, because instructors don't have time to rewrite their courses and redesign their materials. It must be close enough to what's available now to be acceptable, but offer something more to both teacher and student.

□ Can you give me an example of a book that was too different to succeed?

A long time ago I developed an economics book that was completely different from any in use, in a way that seemed to make sense. The standard economics texts were organized around principles of micro- and macroeconomics. This book was built around specific issues of the political economy. I thought, "This book will be meaningful to the students, relevant, and it deals with economic concepts in terms of problems they already know about." I was wrong. Nobody wanted to teach that way. Instructors had years of lectures, course outlines, overhead transparencies, and slides. It was an economic disaster! So the reality is that you can't depart too far from mainstream practice. You want to offer a book that is fresh and mindful, but not too odd. Publishing a book that is simply a knockoff of other books makes no contribution to its field. A book that is eccentric, however, must be regarded as a risky venture.

□ Do you usually go after authors to write introductory-level textbooks, or do they come to you?

Generally, we seek out authors. People don't usually come to us with an idea for a big introductory textbook. We search for them by calling on professors in their offices. We are always asking people who they think are the best teachers in their specialty. Then we go to these instructors (who frequently are far too busy already), and ask them who they think the next best person would be.

□ **Do you receive proposals for textbooks over the transom?**
Proposals for textbooks don't come over the transom as often as those for general trade books do.

□ **What about specialized textbooks?**
Specialized books are normally on more advanced subjects, for junior-, senior-, and graduate-level courses. Professors do frequently seek a publisher for books in their own specialty areas. These books naturally have smaller sales potential, but can fill important niches in a well-rounded publisher's list.

□ **Do you prefer to publish single-author texts or coauthored texts?**
Usually coauthorship is desirable—for division of labor and to have two school affiliations. One normally has a good chance of getting the course adoption for a book at the author's own school. Two authors at very large institutions will help assure a desirable start for sales.

□ **Are authors' credentials important to the sales of books? Do you want full professors, for example?**
You probably won't get a full professor. In this "publish or perish" academic world, a full professor has probably already published a fair amount (although commercial ventures like textbooks may not count toward academic promotions). You're more likely to find as author an assistant or associate professor who is young and ambitious and doesn't mind working all kinds of hours. The author's own educational background and degrees are also important.

□ **Do unknown authors ever publish successful textbooks?**
Unknown people at small schools have certainly written textbooks that turned out to be winners.

□ **What is most important for the sales potential of a textbook?**
The quality of the book. I want an author who really knows the material and can communicate it. That is more important than his or her name. A college author must produce a good manuscript, even if it's with some editorial help.

□ **Do you require proposals from an author you've gone after?**
Yes, but we might walk through the proposal writing exercise together.

□ **What should the proposal include?**
I want a general statement describing the book, an accurate characterization in the prospective author's own words. What is it? What's special about it? What will the approach be?

Next, the proposal should specify the target audience. Who will buy this book? The primary market for a textbook will be a college professor (the decision maker) and a college student (the end purchaser). What course is it designed for? What kind of school will it be used in—university, community college, or vocational-technical institute? Will the reading level be accessible to entering students in any school? I emphasize that it's very important to focus on one clear market, even though it is always tempting to say, "It's a history book, but it's also an architecture book, and it could be used in sociology courses." I say, "Where should we look for your customers, and what should we say to them?"

I need the author's summary of competing books—books for the same course or similar books that serve the same market—with critiques and comparisons. For example, "This book takes a management approach whereas my book will focus on manual skills." This helps us position the book for our marketing and salespeople. Even at the proposal stage, it's important to start establishing the book's own identity. The competition summary should also include all vital statistics of the books in terms of page length, binding, illustrations, and color (if any).

Finally, biographical information about the author should support why he or she is qualified to write the book.

A proposal should include a full outline: a list of the chapters, at least one level of subheadings within each, and a sample chapter or two. A sample chapter for a textbook is important because, in addition to the author's writing style, we want to see how the concepts are delivered and reinforced. Every chapter in a textbook is a lesson, a class. It must be fully rounded. I ask authors *not* to submit chapter 1 as their sample, because the introduction is never typical of the book. You can't really write chapter 1 until the rest of the book is written. Ideally, a sample chapter should come from the middle of the book, so that it assumes a little bit of knowledge and builds on it.

□ How do you define a good proposal?

A good proposal makes it possible for an editor to judge whether the project fills a need in the market and fits into the house's current list. Do we need this book? Can we be successful in marketing it? Will it move us in the strategic direction we have chosen? Can it generate sufficient sales to make it financially profitable for both the author and the company?

I rely on my own first impressions and experience, for rationale, feasibility, and writing style. Then I ask for advice from a half-dozen people I know who are experts in the field and/or teach the course. I ask them to answer some basic questions and mark up the proposal in any way they like. I ask, "Would you assign this text? Are any important topics missing? Are too *many* topics covered?

Could you cover all of this material in one term?" If there seems to be a consensus that this is a good project, or could be with some changes, I will seriously consider going to contract.

If the idea is wonderful and the author is qualified and promotable and could make a real contribution with this book, but does not write well, the editor can decide whether to have a developmental editor work on the manuscript. That is done freelance in most houses today. If a house is going to spend thousands of additional dollars editing and rewriting a book, the sales potential must be large enough to justify it.

□ **What do you want from an author, in addition to a good proposal?**
The author should have a realistic sense of a need his or her book can fill or a contribution it can make. I shy away from people for whom writing a book is an ego trip.

On the other hand, it makes my job easier when an author regards the writing of a book as a commercial venture.

□ **Who is responsible for photographs and illustrations in a textbook?**
Normally illustrations are part of the manuscript and the author provides them. Redrawing charts, graphs, and rough sketches is part of the publisher's production costs. In cases where photographs are wanted and the author cannot supply them, who researches and pays for them is part of the contract negotiations.

□ **Who pays for permissions?**
If passages of text or illustrations from other sources are to be reprinted in the book, it is the author's responsibility to obtain permission from the publisher or author (whichever owns the copyright), and to pay any reprint fees. Obviously this can also be a matter of contract negotiation in special cases, especially where quoted material is a large part of the work, as in an anthology.

□ **Who pays for indexing a textbook?**
Authors prepare their own index, or pay the indexer's fee. I encourage authors to do their own indexing because they know what's important and what students are likely to be looking for.

□ **Who analyzes the market, that is, comes up with the number of students who will take a particular course each year?**
Since this kind of market research is an ongoing process for college editors, the publisher is frequently in the best position to have the information. But the prospective author is the expert on his own institution, and may also have a handle on emerging trends.

□ **Are textbook editors ever agented?**

Rarely.

□ **What about royalties and advances?**

Royalties generally range between 8 percent and 15 percent of the net price of the book. Industry-wide, advances cover the spectrum from none to hundreds of thousands of dollars, depending on the author's wishes, the competitive environment, and the publisher's risk involved with the project. Generally a house expects an author's advance to be earned back in the first year of sales. We want our authors to be collecting royalties by the second year.

□ **What is peculiar to textbook publishing that is not seen in other types of publishing?**

Your customers (college course instructors, who decide which textbook to assign) and your potential authors are identical. An academic who might write a book on supply and demand also teaches economics and might adopt other textbooks that you publish. Our sales reps, in addition to selling our books, are also selling Wiley as a place to publish; our editors, in addition to attracting authors, are also involved in promoting our books.

□ **What are your pet peeves?**

Proposals that say, "No one has ever done this before." My first question is, "Why?" Frequently there's a reason.

□ **Do you mind if authors call you on the phone with an idea?**

Actually, I like it very much. It's my job to know what people are thinking about, and I don't mind giving advice or information because I usually get some back.

□ **Do you have advice for authors in search of a textbook publisher?**

Do some homework on which publishers produce the kind of books you want to write.

Have a track record in your subject area.

Be able to articulate your idea clearly, but be ready to consider alternatives.

Have a realistic idea of a demand your book can fill. You don't have to know the exact dimensions of that demand.

Plan a book that will appear to provide a solution to instructors' teaching problems.

A brief proposal attached to a sample chapter is best. If the proposal interests the editor, he or she can delve into your chapter in depth. It's all right there.

If an author isn't sure of a prospective book's potential, I don't mind a brief letter just saying, "I am thinking of writing a book on restaurant parking lot design. Any interest?"

35

Reference and Test Preparation Books

SATs, Law School, Medical College, Guidance, Career, and College Guides

LINDA BERNBACH, EXECUTIVE EDITOR

Arco
Macmillan General Reference
Macmillan Publishing USA
New York

LINDA BERNBACH has been Executive Editor of Arco since 1989. After graduating from college with a major in journalism, she began her career in magazine publishing as an editor with *Parents Magazine*. Bernbach retired for a few years to start a family and resumed her career in book publishing at Arco in 1972, where she rose to her present position in 1989. Her specialty is test preparation and guidance.

Arco was originally a privately held company that was bought by Prentice Hall, then acquired by Simon & Schuster with the acquisition of Prentice Hall in 1985. Of the seventy-five books Arco publishes each year, many are reprints and revisions of their backlist titles.

☐ **How would you describe Arco's list?**
We're sort of a hybrid. We're educational, but not textbook. We're not trade, we're not school. We're a little of each.

I would not regard any of our books as something the world would know a lot about, but they're very useful books, they sell a lot, and they help people.

□ **Arco is a backlist publisher. What does that mean?**
We have a huge list of books that go on and on and on. Some of our books have been in print since 1937, the very beginning of the company. We have a very extensive revisions program. We constantly update material. We keep updating, revising, and bringing out new editions on a regular two-, three-, or four-year schedule, depending on the nature of the book.

□ **What constitutes a successful reference or test preparation book?**
If it can go on for ten or twelve or fourteen years.

□ **What size markets do these books target?**
It differs. The SAT market is one and a half million kids. With the LSAT, you've got about thirty thousand. There's a big difference in what you can expect to sell.

□ **Do you publish new test preparation books?**
Yes. When new tests come up.

□ **How do you keep current?**
I read all of the literature. For example, I subscribe to the *Chronicle of Higher Education.* We go to guidance counselors' conventions—the National Association of College Admissions Counselors. We go to educational meetings and conventions. Or one of my many contacts says to me, "Did you know that this or that is happening?"

□ **How do you find qualified authors?**
I either go off in search of someone with expertise in a particular area, or someone will come to me say, "I know this is going to happen and I can write a book that will cover it." These writers must have credentials. The man in the street isn't going to able to write SAT math questions. This author is someone who has been teaching math, has been involved in high school level math, and knows what this subject is about.

□ **Do your authors collaborate?**
Usually one person can't handle these books. The person who is qualified and able to write the reading comprehension section is not necessarily qualified and able to write the math section.

□ **Do you deal with agents?**
Ninety percent of what I do is not agented. I work a lot with academics. I find these people myself.

□ **What range of advances can authors of test preparation books expect to be offered?**
Probably from $2,000 to $8,000.

□ **What royalties do you offer?**
Ten percent net. The usual.

□ **This isn't big bucks.**
No. It's a steady, year-after-year kind of income. That's what a backlist publisher is all about. Our backlist is very valuable. People buy our books for years and years and years. A writer could have a steady, small source of income for twenty or thirty years. It's not, in most cases, going to pay for a trip to Tahiti.

□ **Should authors ever call to ask if you would consider an idea before they send a proposal?**
I don't mind that. But I won't consider anything, except in writing. You can call and ask, "Do you do this kind of book?" If we do, and this person sounds qualified to write it, I would be perfectly happy to look at a proposal.

□ **What should a proposal for a test preparation book include?**
The person's qualifications. I want to see some solid teaching or scholastic background. I prefer to hire someone who can write. I require that my authors submit something in writing. I will ask for sample questions, sample explanations, and a couple of sample chapters.

□ **How long does it take you to make a decision, once you receive the proposal?**
We're a large corporation and a lot of people are in on decisions. Decision-making is not as rapid as I would like it to be. It takes two to three months to get a real answer. Anything new needs a lot of input.

□ **Do some authors have misconceptions about writing a book?**
Almost every author grossly underestimates how long it will take to undertake any given project. I'm leery when someone says, "That's really easy. I'll have that to you in three months." It takes much longer. I know that. They don't know that.

Some new authors get bogged down. It's much more difficult and time-consuming to write a book than most people realize. We're always pretty much down to the wire.

□ **Have authors disagreed with you in the development of a book?**
Most people I've worked with have been eager to follow directions and do what was needed to get a good product. There have been a few projects that had to be canceled in the end because we couldn't see eye-to-eye. It wasn't just me. If I

didn't feel the other's work was academically adequate, I'd send it out for review to at least one other very qualified person to back that up.

□ How do you judge a book's worth? You can't be an expert in every field.

If I doubt that a book is done well enough and that the person has enough expertise, I send it to someone who is an expert. I'll seek out a professor. In New York there are lots of people who are well placed in a particular area from whom I can get a review. I'll tackle all of the English parts of a manuscript, because I have the background to do that. I will even attempt math at the high school level. When it gets beyond that, I'll send it out to somebody. For a chemistry manuscript, I'll get a college professor. I have a whole group of people I work with and I'm familiar with, who are always eager to go through and comment on a manuscript.

□ Do you have advice for writers of reference books in their quest to get published?

A well-organized, neat, well-written proposal goes a long way toward making me go further with a project. I am not eager to look at a bunch of handwritten scraps of paper. And I won't.

If a suggestion comes to me in a query letter that is poorly written, I will not consider looking at the manuscript.

36

Educational and Test Preparation and More

GRACE FREEDSON,
MANAGING EDITOR AND DIRECTOR
OF ACQUISITIONS
**Barron's Educational Series, Inc.
Hauppauge, New York**

GRACE FREEDSON, Managing Editor and Director of Acquisitions at Barron's Educational Series, started her career in publicity at Stein and Day Publishers. When her daughter was young, she worked at home as a publicity freelancer, running publicity tours for various publishers. She then became publicity manager at Barron's. She began acquiring books and added the acquisitions aspect to her job. She moved to editorial and now manages a staff of editors. She has been at Barron's since October 1983.

Barron's Educational Series is a privately owned, fifty-two-year-old company. It is relatively small, with just ten editors. Barron's publishes test preparation books, review books, profiles of colleges, and guides for various graduate schools, as well as cookbooks, children's books, language books (audiocassettes for travelers), pet care, business, parenting, retirement, and gardening books. It publishes no fiction, except children's fiction. According to Freedson, you will find "no great American novels at this place."

A very small percentage of the three thousand proposals Barron's receives each year are published. "Much of what we publish is determined from within," says Freedson. "That's when I go out and find authors."

□ **How do you acquire books?**
When we determine what books we want added to the list, I network and seek out appropriate authors. If it's a pet care title, I'll go to some of the organizations or clubs that are pertinent to that breed of cat or dog. Or I'll go to the American Kennel Club or the Cat Fancier's Association to find out who is dealing with that particular breed. Cookbooks usually come to me. With the test preparation books, we determine the next book we want to do, and then I'm hunting all the time. It's a lot of networking.

□ **What percentage of your published books are unsolicited manuscripts and how many are submitted by agents?**
I'd say 5 percent of the manuscripts are unsolicited and 25 percent are from agents.

□ **What is the range of your advances?**
The low is around $2,000. We don't give tremendous advances. I can only recall one advance that went to five figures. Some of our books are done on flat fee basis.

□ **How do you decide on the books you publish?**
I try to balance each season's offerings in the various areas already established. I find two or three pet care titles or two more parenting books, so that I have a balance. It's the same with the test preparation books. Children's books usually come to us. I don't seek out children's books. We get a lot of books from overseas.

□ **What should authors do to get published at Barron's?**
Do your homework and know precisely what our house is publishing.

In recent years, I've seen a marked difference. People are zeroing in exactly on what Barron's publishes. I don't get a lot of proposals for novels or things that are so different from our line. People are doing their homework that way.

□ **How do you feel about multiple submissions?**
I don't have a problem with multiple submissions. I think the time frame for me to give a response to a potential author is so long, that I would hate to think I'm holding somebody up a year waiting for an answer. Sometimes it can take that long just because of the sheer volume. I read everything. Because I take so much time pursuing titles that we want to do, I don't always give a fair amount time to manuscripts that are coming in. I do reading every day.

☐ **What types of books have a better chance of getting published that come in over the transom?**

Cookbooks, children's books, language materials, and types of books that we already publish. I'll give attention right away to unsolicited cookbooks and children's books.

☐ **What do you look for in a complete book proposal?**

The presentation of a nonfiction book should contain a sample table of contents, one sample chapter, and an overview of the project in the cover letter along with the author's credentials for having written that book.

Children's stories are to be sent in their entirety. I do not need to have art accompany it. More often than not, we put an illustrator in place for a project.

On occasion we've had authors and illustrators teamed together. I've had occasion where someone has sent in a story with a particular illustrator and I'll have liked one or the other—you can get turned off a project if you don't like one aspect of it.

☐ **Are your books publicized?**

Publicity is unusual for most of our books. Test preparation books don't lend themselves to that nor do the majority of our books.

☐ **Do you have pet peeves about authors in search of a publisher?**

I have one person who continually submits proposals on onion skin paper. I've had people send in handwritten proposals. It shows that they didn't care. I always wonder how much attention I have to give it on this end.

☐ **Do you have any special advice for authors in search of a publisher?**

It's helpful to send a query letter first because that will save everybody time. You can eliminate a lot of proposals and a lot of time and waiting by sending a query letter with an addressed envelope.

A nice presentation will always draw attention more quickly. A proposal doesn't have to be in fancy packaging, as long as it's typed, double-spaced, and legible.

Patience is something I encourage because this is a very time-consuming process. Once I decide that it's something for us, I have to share it with others here, and then I have to get it evaluated independently. It takes quite a bit of time.

37

Business Books

DAVID CONTI, EDITORIAL DIRECTOR
BUSINESS McGRAW-HILL
Professional Publishing Group
Division of McGraw-Hill, Inc.
New York

DAVID CONTI, Editorial Director of Business McGraw-Hill, majored in English in college. After earning his master's degree, he headed for a New York publishing career with visions of editing the next William Faulkner or Ernest Hemingway. "As with most people in this business," says Conti, "it didn't work out that way." Conti held a variety of editing and production jobs at different houses before becoming an acquisitions editor. After his first business publishing job at Prentice Hall, he spent several years at Boardroom Reports, a business publisher. He then went to Tab Books as head of their business line. When Tab was purchased by McGraw-Hill, Conti and his program were merged with the existing McGraw-Hill business programs. Conti has been editorial director of Business McGraw-Hill since 1990.

McGraw-Hill is over one hundred years old. It is a multimedia publishing and information services company operating throughout the world. It serves markets in education, business, industry, and government. Its operating units include college publishing, school publishing, professional publishing, television stations, trade magazines, *Business Week*, and Standard and Poors.

Business McGraw-Hill receives approximately three thousand proposals each year and publishes one hundred books annually.

□ What are business books?

Books on small business and entrepreneurship, investing and personal finance, marketing, real estate, careers, general management, manufacturing, quality, and training.

□ Do you ever publish first-time authors?

Absolutely. A healthy portion of our books are written by first-time authors.

□ Do you work with agents?

Yes. About half of our authors are agented.

□ Do unagented writers have a good chance of getting published?

Yes.

□ Other publishers told me that unsolicited proposals will not be looked at. Why are you different in that regard?

We take over the transom submissions very seriously. A lot of publishers have a junior person look at slush. We don't. If it's addressed to a specific editor, that editor will open it. If it comes in with no name on it, I'll look at it.

We receive a very different level of unsolicited proposals. The general public isn't knocking on our door. Many of our submissions are from professionals and practitioners in their field as well as from business writers. We don't normally receive proposals from budding novelists, would-be biographers, or poets. That winnows out a lot of writers. We don't have people sending us novels about their dog that died and how it affected their life. Ninety percent of writers are not qualified to write for us because we publish business books.

□ Will you accept phone calls from writers?

We accept phone calls from professionals because we're interested in what they are doing.

□ How do you decide whether a book fits in your list?

We have mission. We don't publish frivolously. One of the company's credos is "serving the need for knowledge." We must feel certain that the book will help someone—help him do his job better or improve his financial situation.

The first question we ask is, "Does it fit?" A proposal for a book on Civil War history, for example, will be returned immediately. We must decide whether the book will fit with our current list and our plans for the future. If it does, then who will use it? Who will buy it? Can we sell enough copies to justify publishing it?

□ Do your books evolve from other people's ideas, or do you find a need and go after an author?

We do both. It's an ongoing process of building a publishing program of different categories of business. In investing, small business, careers, and training, for example, we invite ideas, generate our own ideas, and go out and seek people to work with us.

□ **Are your business books targeted toward a lay audience or to other professionals?**
Some are for a lay audience and some are for professionals. It's diverse. Professional publishing might be a misnomer. Many of our most successful books are for the general public—the investor, the home buyer, the job hunter, or the career changer. We also publish topics that the lay person wouldn't get near—books on quality, manufacturing, and corporate finance that are targeted toward professionals in the business area.

□ **Do books targeted to the lay audience sell more copies?**
They sell more and some of them make a lot more money. But some don't.

□ **Do any of those books become best-sellers?**
In business terms, yes. We don't have books on the *New York Times* best-seller list, but we can sell one hundred thousand or two hundred thousand copies of some books.

□ **Could those books ever make the New York Times best-seller list?**
It's conceivable and something we're working toward. If you follow the nonfiction list, you'll know of *Re-engineering the Corporation*, a long-time best-seller by Michael Hammer and James Champy, published by Harper Business. We could have published a book like that.

□ **Please give me examples of some typical business books that you have published.**
The McGraw-Hill Guide to Starting Your Own Business is an example of a book for the small businessperson. In the area of investing and personal finance, we publish *Graham and Dodd Security Analysis*. But that's not for the individual trying to figure out what to do with an extra $2,000. *Buying Stocks Without a Broker* would be for that person. It's one of our consumer-oriented investing books.

□ **Would you publish a book by a freelance writer who doesn't have professional business qualifications?**
We would, if the idea were strong enough.

□ **Would that writer need a coauthor who has credentials?**
Not necessarily. Our approach is to publish professional people, whether they are stock market investors, advisors to small business, financial advisors, marketing experts, or training consultants. But we do publish professional writers.

□ **What qualifies authors to write business books? What kinds of credentials do they need?**

There is more latitude in the small business category. One of our books, *Financing Your Franchise*, is written by a writer for *Nation's Business Magazine*, an attorney who works with small businesses, and a writer in the business area. These people are not financing or running franchises, but they know all about them. In the investment category, however, we want professionals—people who manage money, write investment newsletters, or work on Wall Street—practitioners. If a freelance writer who does occasional investing wants to write an investment book, it wouldn't be good enough unless that writer comes up with the most wonderful idea I've ever heard of.

□ **What do you want to see in a proposal?**

I have a set of guidelines that ask for the book's "concept and approach"—two or three paragraphs that describe your book, its purpose, approach, and content.

Whom are you writing the book for?

Tell about yourself—your background, your experience, your professional credentials, who your clients are.

Describe the competition. We like to know who authors see as the competition for their book. They are often off the mark, but it gives us some clues as how to proceed. If it's a very narrow specialty and authors really know their business, they can tell us more than we already know. If it's a book for stock market traders, for example, the authors would know the literature as well as we do.

Then we get into technical questions. How long will the book be? When will it be written? Will it require photos?

I like to hear about sales and promotion opportunities. How can you help us get the word out about your book? Do you have media contacts? Can you get endorsements? Will your clients or professional associations be interested in the book? Do you speak regularly for seminars or workshops?

We ask for an outline and a sample chapter.

□ **Do you ever want to see an entire manuscript?**

Yes, but only when we know we're interested to some degree in the project. Because of time constraints, it's often more difficult for us to make a wise judgment on a manuscript than on a proposal. This is probably the hardest thing for writers to understand.

□ **Why is a full manuscript more difficult to make a wise judgment on?**

You need many hours of reading and studying to figure out what a manuscript is about. We'll put that time in once we're more certain we want to publish the work. A proposal will *tell* you what it is and we can hone in and know what we're dealing with much more quickly. In many cases, we'll look at a manuscript. If it looks worthwhile, we might still ask for a proposal.

A book succeeds because many people worked on it—the editor, the publisher, the marketing and production people. They can't all sit down and read the entire book. But they can read through a proposal that pinpoints what they need to know to do their jobs.

□ What kind of money do business writers earn?

Most business publishers base royalties on sales rather than the retail price of the book. Royalties start at 10 percent and go as high as 15 percent of the net price. Advances range from $1,000 to $50,000, based on the individual's need and on what we see as the potential of the book.

□ Do you have pet peeves?

Nothing too serious. The first is someone not understanding the word "no." Occasionally we get someone who persists—that can be a problem.

In probably half of the proposals I read, authors describe the market in terms of the total population of the United States. If it's a book on investing, they'll say, "There are fifty million individual investors in this country and if only 10 percent of them buy this book, we'll sell five million books and we'll all get rich." That shows a lack of understanding of what a book is and who buys books. It takes away from a writer's credibility.

□ Do you have advice for authors in search of a business book publisher?

Writers have to be realistic and try to understand the publishing business. Go into the bookstores and look at the books. That's especially important in business and professional publishing. If you want to write a book on résumés, for example, what books are face out? What books are popular, are being snatched up? Cast your idea against what is in the stores. You will then come to us with a much stronger idea.

A lot of people think they have a unique idea. We ask, "What is the competition?" They answer, "No one has ever written a book like this," which is usually not the case. We need to set your idea up against everything else in the marketplace. Will this idea survive and thrive in the marketplace?

□ Do you have final words about business book publishing?

A lot of people aren't aware of business book publishing. Many people won't read the business section of the *Times*. I have found over the years that the more you know about business, the better off you are in your life. Business is a central force influencing much of what happens to people in this country. If you can understand what's going on in the business world, you can understand and control your own life. You understand about the opportunities and traps along the way, whether you're trying to buy a house, build a career, put a couple dollars in the stock market, fund your kid's college education, or solve a credit card problem. So much in our lives hinges on a knowledge of how business works. People should pay more attention.

38

Sensational Nonfiction and True Crime

PAUL DINAS, EXECUTIVE EDITOR

Pinnacle Books
Imprint of Kensington Publishing Corp.
New York

PAUL DINAS, Executive Editor at Pinnacle Books, was an English major in college. He was bitten by the publishing bug when, after graduation, he worked for a vanity publisher on Long Island. When Dinas learned everything he needed to know about book publishing, he headed to Manhattan. He worked at St. Martin's Press in trade editorial for four years, then went to Avon Books. He freelanced for a while, helped start a new imprint at Harlequin Books, worked in book packaging for two years, and was hired by Pinnacle in May 1989. He started as senior editor, specializing in male fiction. At that time, the true crime craze was heating up but, according to Dinas, no one at Pinnacle had the stomach for it. Because of Dinas's strong interest in the area, he became the true crime editor. Dinas was promoted to executive editor in 1992.

Pinnacle Books was privately held until the late 1980s, when it went bankrupt. The company and its assets were bought by Walter Zaccharias, founder and owner of Zebra Books. Pinnacle became a second imprint under the Kensington umbrella company. Pinnacle publishes 120 mass market books a year.

☐ **Tell me about Pinnacle's book list.**
Pinnacle's book list is small, with a commercial mix of fiction and nonfiction. The nonfiction list includes original mass market books that are tied into sensa-

tional topics—celebrity biographies, true crime, or eccentric topics that we consider media-worthy, like an instant book on Tonya Harding or a book on the trial of Lorena Bobbitt—and other popular nonfiction books, such as humor collections or reference works and film or current events that are not sensational, just commercial.

□ **Tell me about instant books. Who thinks them up? How do they come about? How long do they take to produce?**
It happens in roughly two ways. Someone may pitch us an idea for an instant book. That's usually from a packager or an agent with a writer who is particularly well versed in the topic or has a particular angle for an instant book. Most often it comes from an idea generated in-house and we find a writer with experience on that topic.

From contract to distribution, production takes about three weeks. Maybe a month.

□ **What about the quality of a book written that quickly?**
It depends on the writer. Many writers of these books are journalists. They are used to writing fast and clean. The majority of the books are accessible and good. We're not looking for stylized pieces or great works of literature. We're looking for clear, concise writing that will communicate the whole story as directly as possible to the reader.

□ **Do you need a proposal for an instant book?**
Yes. If it's our idea, we need a proposal from a writer to show that he can pull it together and structure it. If it's a writer's idea, we usually get it from a proposal.

□ **How do you acquire most of your books?**
We acquire many books from literary agents. Occasionally, we buy from an unknown or first-time author. If someone has never written a book before, but has a personal connection to a very sensationalized story, I'll often buy the story and work with the author on the writing. We also come up with our own ideas and find someone to write the book.

□ **Do you ever publish proposals that come in over the transom?**
All the time. About 7 percent. The percentage is low because the majority of the material we get is either not commercial or poorly written.

□ **Do you look for specific criteria for authors of sensational nonfiction or true crime?**
I don't look for any specific criteria although it helps if they've had a journalism background because (1) they know about deadlines; (2) they know how to do research and interviews; (3) they know the legalities of getting releases for

pictures and interviews and are less likely to use material that might be libelous or actionable.

□ **What do you want included in a proposal for a true crime or sensational nonfiction book?**
A good solid proposal should be about twenty pages. If the writer is unknown, I want two or three sample chapters along with the proposal.

Ideally the proposal should include these elements.

A strong concept statement in the beginning—what the project is in a page or less, so that I get a very clear sense of the book.

Ten to fifteen pages telling the story, from start to finish, with names, dates, and places. The proposal should convey the overall structure of how the writer intends to communicate the story to the reader.

A market overview—the competition for this kind of book and other successes of similar books.

And finally, a profile of the author and why he or she feels particularly well suited to write this book.

□ **Do you ever want to see the completed manuscript?**
Yes. If someone has the whole book written, it will save time to submit it with a complete synopsis or outline. A writer's time is valuable. Wasting time is the worst thing a writer can do, and I believe query letters and proposals are a big waste of time. It's very inefficient. I prefer to have as complete a submission as possible to review for acquisition.

□ **How much money do authors earn who write true crime books?**
Advances range from $3,000 to five figures. Royalties range from 6 percent to 8 percent and can escalate to 10 percent of the retail price of the book.

□ **How do you decide on the number of copies to print?**
It's based on the story, the competition for the story, the position on the list, the strength of the cover treatment, and the track record of the author. The range in sensational nonfiction is anywhere from 50,000 to 350,000.

□ **What makes a winning true crime story stand out from a loser?**
The best true crime illuminates some darker side of humanity. It gives us access to the thought process and the world of the criminal, the sociopath, and the psychopath that we lay people do not normally have. It teaches us about the depths of depravity and the social forces that produce those depths. It also can show how the justice system works or doesn't work.

The best true crime is socially significant. It has a social conscience and it both analyzes and sensationalizes the nature of the story itself.

I look for visceral killing, multiple victims, and the unique nature of the crime.

It's always interesting to have a woman killer and a strong psychosexual element to the crime.

Hands-on killing is more commercial than paid assassinations or contract killings. Crimes that I call white bread domestic crimes, such as poisoning for insurance purposes, fixing the brakes so the husband or wife will die, or killing an aged grandparent, do not usually have enough texture or intrinsic interest to hold a whole book together commercially. What people love to read about is the personal involvement of the killer. The idea of a housewife actually driven to stabbing or taking out the eyes of her husband because of his abuse is a lot more exciting than her having paid her next door neighbor to kill him with a hunting gun.

Children killing children is a very strong topic. Adults killing children is also interesting.

□ **Give me an example of one of your typical true crime books.**
Cruel Sacrifice, by Aphrodite Jones, a story about teenage lesbians who kidnapped and tortured a twelve-year-old girl, then burnt her alive, in Indiana.

□ **Is true crime a relatively new genre?**
It's a relatively new genre if you're referring to the commercial attention and success it's achieved. It has really gotten hot in the past four or five years. However, as a genre, it's been around for decades.

□ **Why have true crime books become so popular?**
There are a lot of reasons. True crime gives the lurid pleasure of seeing or reading about something that is hideously outside most people's normal lives, similar to the excitement of watching an auto accident. Also, I think people like to see justice done. They have so little control of the system and things that go on in their lives that when people see a story about a heinous crime that eventually ended with the incarceration or execution of the criminal, it makes them feel good that they live in a country in which the system works and they can feel protected.

□ **Is there a formula for writing true crime?**
The formula usually depends on the crime itself. However, there are several aspects that most true crime books include: the description of the crime itself; the police investigation and eventual arrest of the criminal; the discovery process of the criminal's motivation, background, and past record; the trial sequence and conviction; and an epilogue that can follow the effects of the crime on the families of the victim, the community, and the law enforcement professionals involved in the case.

True crime is a book-length report and analysis of a specific crime. Original research, interviews, and personal insights aside, the true crime writer's primary responsibility is to present the case as accurately and dramatically as possible.

□ **There is now a larger market for true crime and sensational nonfiction. What were these writers writing before?**
Many were working journalists who never wrote a full-length book. Some were novelists who decided to try their hands at true crime. Many never wrote books, had this talent to investigate and communicate a story, but didn't have a vehicle. Now they have the true crime genre, which gives them a showcase for their ability and their talent in an area that may also offer them financial security.

□ **Do you offer writers travel money?**
No. They pay for travel out of their advance. But there are other expenses. Authors have to make dozens of long distance phone calls, obtain trial transcripts, which can run as much as $6 a page, and purchase photographs, which can run into hundreds of dollars.

When writers want to do a true crime book, they have to think about all that when negotiating their contract.

□ **Do all true crime books have pictures?**
Yes. Some publishers publish true crime in hardcover without pictures. And they usually don't succeed. True crime is a tabloid market, and tabloid's meat and potatoes are pictures. The first thing people do when they pick up one of these books is to flip through the picture section. If you don't have a picture section, it's very frustrating and people probably won't buy the book.

□ **When you say tabloid, one thinks of lower-quality writing. Aren't there some true crime books, such as Truman Capote's *In Cold Blood*, which are of very high literary quality?**
In Cold Blood was not true crime as we have come to describe it. It's "faction," as was *The Executioner's Song* by Norman Mailer, both brilliant exercises in blending fiction and nonfiction.

There have been some true crime books that are more personal books, and are not actual reportorial accounts. Some writers, like Jack Olsen, Joe McGinnis, and Vincent Bugliosi, often write big, complicated books, whose voice is not strictly reportorial.

□ **Joe McGinnis's involvement with the central figure of *Fatal Vision* is legendary. Do other authors become so involved?**
Yes. We did a reprint of a Simon & Schuster book called *Daddy's Girl* by Clifford Irving, in which Irving actually became a witness during the trial because of his own investigation of the murder.

□ **What sparks your interest in a proposal for sensational nonfiction?**
A proposal for sensational nonfiction must involve a subject that has generated a great deal of press coverage, but has not been written about in a book. Celebrity biographies, exposés of society people, or controversial current events are a few of the topics that fall into this category.

□ **Do you evaluate the author of a celebrity biography to verify his or her connection?**
Yes. I always say to writers, "This is a great story, but how can you give it to me? What access do you have?" In terms of celebrities, access is everything. If you have access to a source that no one else has, okay, we can talk. But if you're going to just write a clip and paste, anyone can do that.

□ **What if writers say they have access, but it falls through after a contract has been signed?**
It's very difficult to access people's claims. You meet with people, talk to them, talk to their agent, they give you all of the supporting information, they say they can deliver this, this, and this. You want to believe them because it's very commercial. You draw up a contract. Delivery day comes. "Where's that nude picture you promised?" I'll ask. "Oh, I had a little problem getting that," the writer responds. "Did you talk to the brother?" I ask. "Well, he wouldn't talk to me," the writer responds. The manuscript is unacceptable and we won't publish it, or we publish it at a much lower level than we wanted to. It can be very disappointing.

□ **Do your authors do big-time media blitzes—talk shows, and the like?**
Yes. We get a lot of attention because there's a huge, voracious need for these stories on magazine shows and on the regular circuits. There used to be a rule in book publicity that original paperbacks did not get reviewed and did not get any kind of publicity. That is not the case now because of the need for true crime and sensational book properties. It doesn't matter anymore whether it's hardcover or not because people are looking for the story.

□ **What makes a successful author for public relations and media?**
The most successful authors in the PR realm are those who can deliver principals in the story to the TV shows. Audiences are not as interested in the author as they are in the people who actually underwent the experience.

□ **Do you have pet peeves about authors?**
Writers who say, "I'll write the book, then get the pictures." The pictures often take longer to get than writing the book. Authors must be aware from the beginning that if they're entering into this genre, they have to be gathering the

pictures as they write the text. Pictures are almost equal to the commercial value of the text.

□ **Do you have advice for authors who want to get a true crime or sensational nonfiction book published?**
First and foremost, be very market savvy. It's very important to pick the right story. Watch the magazine shows and pay attention to the news. Hook your computer into a wire service if you can.

Assess the amount of time and effort it's going to take to write a whole book.

Look for local crime, a crime you can drive to and drive back at night. Your overhead will be cut by 70 percent. It will cost you a lot of money to fly and live someplace for six weeks doing research. You should be careful about your overhead and about the time you're going to spend on the project.

Be very careful about your source material and getting releases from your source.

Look at the structure of similar books. Study the way successful books are written. That will be very helpful in constructing your own book. Read a lot of true crime and get a sense of the different kinds of structures and different areas you can go into with your particular story—what's appropriate and what's not appropriate.

There is strong film interest in this area. Writers who have access to a principal in the story should try to get exclusive rights to the story, for the possibility of selling it to film companies.

39

Mystery/Crime Fiction

The Plot Thickens—But How?

SARA ANN FREED, EXECUTIVE EDITOR,

MYSTERIOUS PRESS

SENIOR EDITOR FOR WARNER BOOKS, INC.

Imprint of Warner Books, Inc.

New York

SARA ANN FREED, Executive Editor of Mysterious Press, majored in history at a small religious college. Her first publishing job was with a religious publisher; her next position was with the Harper & Row rights department in New York. Freed was asked to edit mysteries at her next job as subsidiary rights director at Walker & Co. The first book she bought, *Bay Song Murder* by Will Harriss, won an Edgar. She had always enjoyed reading mystery novels, but now she found a career. Freed's editing specialty is crime novels.

Mysterious Press publishes mystery/crime fiction. They rarely publish romantic suspense, espionage, horror, or true crime. It was founded by bookseller Otto Penzler, owner of the Mysterious Book Shop in New York. The press was later sold and now is an imprint of Warner Books.

Mysterious Press publishes three to four hardcovers and three to four paperbacks each month.

☐ **What should a complete proposal for a mystery novel include?**
I don't like proposals. I prefer to see an entire manuscript from first novelists or people whose work I don't know. It's not like a cookbook or a diet book. You

really have to have a sense of how the writer deals with the beginning, middle, and end.

☐ **Is there a formula for a winning mystery novel?**
Never. Absolutely not. If you look at the books that have won a major award, there's nothing that you can put your finger on and say, "Aha, that made it a winning book."

☐ **What is the criterion for a successful crime novel, a story that people respond to?**
A really wonderful voice. No one can explain it. Margaret Maron's *Bootleggers Daughter* won the Edgar this year. From the very first page I said, "This is really special."

☐ **How would you describe such a book to your marketing people, to help them understand why and how you have responded to it?**
It has to do with the use of language, the use of prose, and how the character comes alive. How the author integrates plot, setting, character, and prose, and makes it special. I guess that's how you can define voice.

We get in so many manuscripts in which the prose is perfect, the grammar is perfect, the spell-check works on the computer—but the prose is flat and tired and dead. If you read all day long or take a stack of manuscripts home on the weekend, the good one just pops out.

☐ **Is the first paragraph the key to readers when they pick up the book?**
Very often it is. It was when I read Joseph Loenig's *Floater* in manuscript. Even more so, I think, than the title. People often say, "That's such a special title." I think that books can have fairly pedestrian titles and nobody minds if the book is good.

☐ **What are you not looking for in a mystery?**
I'm not a good puzzle person. I don't care so much about what happens. When I go to the movies, I'm always punching my husband, asking him, "What happened? What happened?" He says, "You're supposed to be the mystery editor; you're supposed to know what happened." I care what happens to people and I care about justice.

The thing that I'm always interested in is strong character and setting. I've always been nuts for the Tony Hillerman books. I love Ellis Peters' medieval Brother Cadfael books. I think that out of characters comes the puzzle. I'm interested in why people do what they do and why people commit crime. The straight puzzle books don't do it for me.

□ **Give me an example of a writer who incorporated all of this.**

A new writer, Abigail Padgett, took a character who is manic-depressive and made her fun, interesting, and engaging. She used the California San Diego desert in a really fresh way.

□ **Must mystery novels reflect the real world?**

It helps, but it's not altogether necessary. If you think about all the people who still like traditional crime novels, with a puzzle-type element, you know that they are reading for entertainment, to escape the real world.

□ **What is the best way to market a book?**

Good reviews sell books. But the biggest tool is word of mouth. Think about how often people have told you to read a certain book. The publisher could do anything—take out ads, hang banners from blimps—and it wouldn't have done any good. It's individual reader's enthusiasm that makes all the difference.

□ **Does the manuscript go through a lot of red tape before you make a decision?**

Surprisingly not. If I like a book, I ask William Malloy, the editor in chief, to read it. Then we talk about it at weekly editorial meetings.

□ **What is the range of advances offered to mystery writers?**

From zero to infinity. I've heard of some houses that give no advances. If you're a Mary Higgins Clark or Robert Parker, the sky's the limit.

□ **Do mystery writers need credentials?**

None. Absolutely none. I just bought a book from a woman who told me she never graduated from high school. We receive many manuscripts from lawyers, doctors, journalists, and teachers. I've always have had the feeling that mysteries are one kind of leisure fiction read by busy professionals. Sometimes they imagine themselves writing one. But a lawyer who writes a legal thriller who can get the law right isn't necessarily a fiction writer.

The best mysteries come from people who read and love mysteries. This sounds too obvious, but it's true.

I get mysteries from people who say, "I'm a professional freelance writer and I see you're publishing mysteries." These are people who do diet books, how-to's of any kind, science fiction books. Those are the least successful mystery writers because they have no passion for the field.

□ **Were mysteries always big business?**

In the early 1980s, when I first started editing mysteries, the mystery field was deader than a door nail. I remember trying to send some of my books that I was doing at Walker to Bantam, to interest them in paperback rights. They'd say, "We're not interested. We're not even going to open the box."

Now, of course, Bantam is one of the biggest publishers of mysteries in the business. Since then, there's been a big explosion of mystery books. You might notice how many mystery books make the *New York Times* best-seller list. There are nearly one hundred bookstores that specialize in mysteries. Every bookstore has a mystery section.

□ What are your pet peeves?

Drug plots. I'm really sick of drug plots.

I'm getting a little tired of child abuse in every book. Somebody can write a book about underwater snorkeling, and they'll manage to put a child abuse plot. Not that I'm diminishing the seriousness of the problem. Too many writers don't care about fresh plots and new ideas.

□ Do you have advice for mystery writers who are searching for a publisher?

Find out what each publisher is doing.

Get a good agent.

Go to one of the crime fan conventions. The biggest one is called Boucher-con. It's held every year in October. There are also several good regional ones. One is held on the West Coast every February. Another is held on the East Coast every November. Visit dealers' rooms to see what kinds of books are being published. Sit in panels to see what other mystery writers talk about, how they got started in the field.

Other mystery writers are a good source of help. It's surprising how generous mystery writers are to newcomers. They often introduce a newcomer to their publisher or agent, they'll read a new writer's manuscript, and give them blurbs if they like the book.

In fact, mystery writers are my favorite people.

40

Science Fiction and Fantasy

BRIAN THOMSEN

DIRECTOR OF BOOKS AND PERIODICALS,

EXECUTIVE EDITOR OF BOOKS

ASSOCIATE PUBLISHER: *DRAGON, DUNGEON,* AND

AMAZING MAGAZINES

TSR, Inc.

Lake Geneva, Wisconsin

BRIAN THOMSEN was an English and psychology double major, and a political science minor in college. "This provided me with the cover story to my parents that I was contemplating law school," he explains. During the summer between his junior and senior years, he did an executive internship at Warner Books. The student internship turned into a full-time job after graduation. He edited trivia books during the trivia boom and worked on movie tie-ins. When Warner began publishing science fiction and fantasy, the entire program fell into Thomsen's hands. He worked at Warner Books from 1980 until 1992, when he moved to TSR. Thomsen is director of books and periodicals, executive editor of books, and associate publisher of *Dragon, Dungeon,* and *Amazing* magazines.

TSR, (Tactical Strategy Supports) publishes a mix of 50 percent science fiction and 50 percent fantasy books. In its early days, TSR published material to aid in military war games. The founder of the company then developed the Dungeons and Dragons game, which started off as a small pamphlet, grew into a complete set of rule books, and then became a nationwide craze. "From Dungeons an Dragons we go the entire field called fantasy role playing, which has given birth to numerous other incarnations," explains Thomsen. Out of this grew the book program.

□ **What separates a science fiction and fantasy from a mainstream book?**

Mainstream books are all those that sell to the widest amount of people. *Jurassic Park* and *Andromeda Strain* are mainstream science fiction novels. Because they became very popular and are solidly based in a world not that dissimilar to our own, say ten years in the future, the publishers were able to market those books as mainstream. That increased their possible reader base. Likewise, Stephen King, no matter what he writes, is always going to be considered mainstream now. But he has written fantasies. A book called *The Eyes of the Dragon* is an example. Because he reaches out to so many people, he is mainstream.

There are also successful mainstream books that are bad science fiction or fantasy novels. Margaret Atwood's *The Handmaid's Tale* is a bad science fiction book. P. D. James' *The Children of Men* is a bad science fiction book. But both of them are fine mainstream books because they have used the trappings of science fiction as allegory and metaphor. The scenario that Atwood projects in *The Handmaid's Tale* defies credibility. James' science fictional underpinnings of what caused society to get where it was don't have any basis in the science she refers to. That doesn't bother a lot of mainstream. So it is possible to write a successful mainstream book that is a bad science fiction book.

□ **Is science fiction and fantasy one classification? When you think of science fiction, do you always add fantasy?**

Everybody on the outside does. Everybody on the inside looks at them as two different things.

□ **What is the difference between science fiction and fantasy?**

Science fiction is either future-based or involves a change in a rule of science. For example, *Frankenstein* is science fiction because a man uses science to create a living being.

Fantasy, on the other hand, involves a departure from reality. In fantasy there is acceptance of the belief that there is a quality of specialness that can usually result in such things as enchantment or magic. James Gunn probably summed it up best when he said, "Science fiction is based on the precept that everybody is equal and the scientist is able to acquire specialized knowledge so that he can do something that somebody else can't do because they don't have that knowledge. But if they had that knowledge, they would be able to do it. Fantasy is based on the fact that there are certain people who are special. Some people can do magic. Other people can't do magic. Not everybody is an elf; therefore, there is a difference."

More than that, science fiction is usually based on an extrapolation from reality. We don't necessarily know what life is going to be like in the future but we do have the basis of belief. For example, if we were going to have a story about Pluto (the planet) now, we know the scientific conditions of Pluto. The story would have to deal with those conditions. In fantasy, nine-tenths of the worlds are created from whole cloth. There is a noticeable departure from reality. This departure can be as simple as the existence of elves and fairies or the existence of somebody who can snap their fingers and make a rabbit jump out of a hat, for real, not in a trick.

□ **What are the criteria for a winning science fiction and fantasy story?**
Number one: it has to have a certain page-turning quality—a concept that from page one is intriguing enough to make you want to go on. In most cases we are dealing with a scenario that is alien to or one step beyond our normal, everyday life. The reader has to be hooked and brought along fairly quickly.

Number two: not only does it have to be intriguing, but it has to be believable from step one. This is not to say that the reader has to believe what is going on in the story. But the reader has to believe that the story makes sense. The reader doesn't have to believe that there are such things as elves, fairies, or beings from the planet Mars, but he does have to believe that if there were such beings, this is what they would be doing.

Number three: there has to be a degree of originality. One of the running jokes at writers' workshops is that there are certain themes that have been done so many times that they can't be done again unless by an expert, because they just don't make sense. For example, the idea of two people surviving a nuclear holocaust and starting a new world together as Adam and Eve (at the end of the story you find out their names) has been done to death. It's not going to work again. The story about a man who is fighting for the rest of humanity only to find out that he himself is a robot has been done too many times. Likewise, the man who has gone back in time to kill his own father and then ceases to exist. These are all scenario stories that are usually the first ones that a beginning writer jumps on. The problem is that everybody has done them before. There has to be that degree of originality.

□ **Is there a formula for writing science fiction and fantasy?**
I have to go back to my own schooling. I've done short stories. For me, it all comes out of watching "Twilight Zone" when I was younger. Rod Sterling taught the perfect short story format: three acts—beginning, middle, and end—dealing with only enough information that could be conveyed and understood within a confined amount of time. So if there's a formula, that, in my mind, is the formula.

□ **Do you deal with first-time, unagented writers?**
All the time. We also deal with agents. The ratio is about 60–40, unagented-agented. I buy books out of the slush pile. I also buy books from people at writers'

workshops. I help them nurture the book along until it's ready. And, quite frankly, I buy books by calling people and saying, "Remember, you wanted to do that book? I'd like to see it. Do you want to do it?" I also get books from recommendations of other people.

□ **Does a first-time, unagented author have a better chance with a publisher?**
I think a first-time author has a better chance with somebody out of New York if he or she is able to find the right niche. An example is a feminist science fiction novel that is in reality a metaphor for women in the 1990s. Whether it's agented or unagented doesn't really matter. It's not right for the TSR list. Having an agent helps you rule out places where it wouldn't be right. The agent basically saves you the amount of postage that you would waste in sending it where it wouldn't work.

□ **Do you want a proposal or an entire manuscript?**
It's better to start off with a detailed proposal, but the author should be prepared to send off the whole manuscript.

For a novel, I usually want a detailed outline of three to four pages and a writing sample of three chapters in consecutive order. But again, it's with the knowledge that if I want the rest of the book, it's available. Some people send the entire manuscript, even if you only ask for the chapters and the outline. I will probably get to the chapters and outline faster than I will to the whole manuscript.

□ **How does a proposal for a science fiction/fantasy book differ from one for a mystery or a romance? What will help the writer sell the book?**
There are a few things that help you sell your science fiction or fantasy novel. That which is special or different about your book can be conveyed in the proposal. You are not just selling plot, you are also selling background and a degree of originality that you are bringing to your new creation, whether it is on the lines of super science or the new fantasy world that you have created. Both of these are selling points that you don't have if you're selling romance, western, history, or a mystery. If there is a way that you can capture the originality, it helps sell your book.

□ **How do you decide that there is place for a book in your publishing program?**
There's only one way to sum it up: by the gut. I was at a convention and somebody from the audience raised his hand at a "Meet the Editor" panel and asked, "What gives you the right to decide what gets published and what doesn't

get published?" I thought about it for a moment. I couldn't say that I have a degree in English because a lot of people have degrees in English. I couldn't say because I have read the entire works of Stephen King. The answer became quite clear. The answer was, "That's what I'm paid to do. When I cease to be good at doing that, people will stop paying me to do it." There is no way to sum up what the parameter is because it all comes out of your gut.

□ Do writers of science fiction and fantasy books need credentials?

I have bought science fiction and fantasy books from housewives, from engineers, and from teachers. The thing that strikes me is that these people were all readers. They don't sit in a vacuum to create their own work without outside influences.

I buy from people who are familiar with both fields. Some of them have extensive world-building experience, from having read a lot, having done a lot of gaming, or having an advanced degree in physics. They give credentials to their work that is not apparent in the work of, let's say, a lay person who decides to sit down and write a science fiction novel and has never studied anything. In fact, I have received proposals from people who have published other books and have decided to try their hand at science fiction because it looks like it sells. I get a proposal that may look like a good book, but it's not a good science fiction book. There's something that doesn't work because it has been done many times before and there isn't the internal sense of why things happen—they're asking the reader to suspend too much disbelief.

□ What kind of money do science fiction and fantasy writers earn?

Our advances are on par with most paperback advances in New York. On a first novel in New York for science fiction or fantasy, the advance is anywhere from $3,000 to $5,000. The royalties are normally 6 percent, breaking to 8 percent based on the book's cover price. Our royalties are slightly lower, but we have several things in our contract that are more equitable to the author.

□ Do you have pet peeves about authors?

During the presentation of the manuscript, the manuscript speaks for you. If there is any reason given to me not to read a manuscript, I won't. If your dot matrix is too pale or everything is single-spaced—that's enough reason for me to just give it a scan and reject it. It is unreasonable for an author to expect an editor who doesn't know his work to go to any great pains to be impressed.

I've also had authors track me down and call me at home. They should never do this. Writers don't have definable office hours. Editors do. Editors are reachable when they are in the office of the company they're working for. They are not reachable at home unless the author is given special dispensation, and that is usually done on a personal level between the editor and author. It is very, very bad form for a writer to find out an editor's home phone number and call him or her there. If you can't get him Friday afternoon, you have to wait until Monday.

Keeping an open mind is always the best tact for a writer. Indeed, what the editor may have asked for originally might not have been the right thing. It is through ongoing dialect that both author and editor can come together and figure out what the right thing is. An author has to realize that threats are not going to get him or her anywhere. You can be insistent without being unreasonable. It is better to continue to ask questions, rather than to say, "I disagree with you." The longer you talk, the more you will get out of it.

□ **Do you have words to the wise for authors in search of a publisher, especially science fiction and fantasy writers?**
Know what publishers publish. Go to the bookstores and see what is on the shelves. What is selling? It's a lot easier to find a home if you know that you're going to be invited into the neighborhood.

You have to be aware of what is in the marketplace today. For a while I was receiving a lot of proposals for Middle Eastern fantasy and science fiction. There was a flurry of them at one time, but they didn't sell. If you keep aware of market trends, you are more likely to decide whether your project is marketable.

My best advice is to go to bookstores on a regular basis and keep up with what's out there right now.

□ **Do you have other advice for writers?**
Many books are successful because the author was at the right place at the right time. The author must be available to turn out something very fast. An editor may say, "I have an opening in this anthology but somebody else didn't come through. Can you do something?" One has to be ready at all times.

You have to enjoy writing. There is no reason in the world to suffer through the writing of a book. If you're not enjoying it, you're probably doing the wrong thing.

41

Adult Category Romance Books

ISABEL SWIFT, EDITORIAL DIRECTOR
Silhouette Books
New York

ISABEL SWIFT was an English major in college. "When I tried to determine what I wanted to do after graduation," says Swift, "I decided that I needed to answer the question, 'What do I do well that I like doing that someone would pay me to do?' And I decided to find work in romance publishing—I loved the books, I read them, and someone out there was getting *paid* to read them, and that someone should be me." Swift took a job at Pocket Books in New York as an editorial assistant, rose to assistant editor, then moved to the subsidiary rights department before being promoted to assistant director of Richard Gallen Books, a line of romances distributed by Pocket Books. In 1982 she moved to Silhouette Books as an associate editor, where she worked her way up to "running the office." She has been editorial director since 1991. Her specialty is women's fiction and romance.

The Silhouette imprint includes five lines of category contemporary novels—*Silhouette Romance, Silhouette Desire, Silhouette Special Edition, Silhouette Intimate Moments, and Silhouette Shadows*—the Harlequin historical line, several short story collections, and two continuity programs, The Loop and Montana Mavericks. Silhouette Books began in 1980 with Silhouette *Romance*. In 1984 a wholly owned subsidiary of Harlequin Enterprises, Ltd. bought the Silhouette imprint from Simon & Schuster. Harlequin has offices throughout the world. "Women of every nationality enjoy romance," says Swift.

□ What are category romance books?

Category romances are part of the larger genre of romance novels. Broadly, romance can be defined as anything with a romance in it. A category romance is focused on the developing relationship between one man and one woman and that relationship's successful resolution—a happy ending. With Silhouette and Harlequin romances, we create lines of books. Each line has a set number of books per month, a cover that has consistent elements, and stories that promise a certain type of reading experience. We publish six books a month in *Silhouette Romance, Desire, Special Edition* and *Intimate Moments,* two books a month in *Shadows,* and four books a month in Historicals. Historicals are not category romances.

Each of our lines has a different cover style and package and is directed to a different readership or mood. *Silhouette Romances,* for example, are traditional contemporary love stories. They are about two hundred pages long, and the covers are white with a square illustration of the main characters. *Silhouette Desires* are modern, sexy stories with a red border around the art. *Silhouette Special Editions* are longer, more complex love stories with wraparound art and an arch across the top. *Intimate Moments* have elements of adventure, suspense, and glamour, and are minimally branded with a dark pink bar. *Silhouette Shadows* are stories about the dark side of love, with a black and bronze band across the top of the art. These consistent elements across a line promise a reader quality, and make the books category romances.

□ How does category romance publishing differ from other romance fiction?

Harlequin and Silhouette publish over 725 *original* paperbacks a year, more titles if you count reprints. I don't think anybody else does that.

□ What are your criteria for a winning category romance?

A story that speaks to me and meets our readers' expectations. When a reader buys a Silhouette book, she expects to get a love story. If you write a book that doesn't have romance in it, it's not going to work for us.

□ Is there a formula?

There is no formula, but there is a requirement to meet reader expectations. Readers expect a satisfying end result, but there's no requirement on how to get there. The writer must create the right problem and then come up with the right solution. Certain key ingredients are necessary, but it is up to the author to figure out how they are mixed together.

□ How do you guide new writers?

We have tip sheets with information about the lines and ask that writers send a self-addressed, stamped envelope to receive guidelines. Tip sheets include information on how to write and submit to *Silhouette Romance, Desire, Special Editions, Intimate Moments,* and *Shadows* lines, as well as Harlequin Historicals; required word lengths; levels of sensuality; and submission procedures. To understand what readers are looking for, we recommend that authors read the books.

□ **Do you define how far the level of sensuality is allowed to go?**
Silhouette Romances are traditional and don't have lovemaking prior to marriage. The *Desires, Special Editions, Intimate Moments, Shadows,* and the Historical lines include sensuality, though it depends on the relationship and the situation the writer has created as to what happens, when it happens, and how that works into the story.

□ **Why are romance books so popular?**
Romances are written to totally sweep a reader away, to capture her imagination, and to be a compelling and fun reading experience. Harlequin and Silhouette are in the entertainment business. Our commitment is to entertain our readers and make them happy. They come from all walks of life. Many are educated and have high-powered jobs. Their lives are demanding. They want to have a reading experience that they can just enjoy, one that gives something *to* them, rather than demands something *from* them. If you have a tough job, in or out of the home, you probably don't want to put up your feet and read *Moby Dick.* What you really want to do is relax, refresh, recoup, and regenerate yourself, and Silhouette and Harlequin books do that for our readers.

□ **What is the age and educational level of your readers?**
Romance readers run the spectrum from age 11 to 101. Close to half have attended or graduated from college, and over half are employed part-time or full-time.

□ **Has your readership changed through the years, and has your focus changed because of that?**
The readership has changed because category romances are written by, for, and about women. In the past decade we've seen enormous changes in the opportunities, challenges, decisions, compromises, and options that women have had to face. Silhouette books reflect that.

□ **Why, in this day of so-called gender equality, aren't there men's romantic fiction books?**
The sexes should have equal opportunity, but they are simply not the same. Men are different from women, and men's entertainment fiction is different. Genres men often read to relax are action/adventure, espionage, mystery, or science fiction.

□ Who are your writers?

Our author base is made up of women from all walks of life—lawyers, architects, teachers, computer programmers, nurses, homemakers. There are women who have high school degrees, others with advanced degrees. Our writers can be single, married, divorced, or widowed, but all love the romance genre and are committed to and respect the readers.

□ Do writers of category romance books need credentials?

No. The vital requirement is simply a good book that's going to appeal to our readers. A real understanding and love for the genre, a commitment to their work, a commitment to being professional, and taking themselves seriously are the important credentials writers need.

The incredible thing about category romance is that a brand new author can be published successfully next to an established author. The lines we publish are strongly branded. A reader recognizes and trusts a particular line, and she's willing to take a chance on a new author if the story looks good.

□ What do you recommend to authors who want to publish a category romance?

Our key recommendation is to try to understand the reader and what she's looking for. Many Silhouette authors have been successful because they started off as readers. They have a gut understanding of what the reader is looking for, and that's what they write.

□ What is your submission policy for unagented authors?

We ask that they submit a query letter that indicates what line they're interested in writing for, why they think their project is special, any publishing experience they may have had, and a two-page synopsis of the story that gives us a clear idea of plot and characters, and a self-addressed, stamped envelope. We'll look at that and may ask to see more.

Our door is always open to unagented authors. Since we instituted the query letter system, our acquisition of new authors has increased.

□ What chance does a first-time author have in getting published with Silhouette Books?

We usually publish fifteen to twenty-five authors who have not been previously published each year. We are always looking for talented new authors.

□ How do you find new authors?

We find them from agents (about half of our authors are represented by agents), from query letters, from contests, from conferences, from all over.

□ **Is it advantageous for a category romance writer to retain an agent?**
A good book will sell without an agent, and a bad book won't sell with an agent. At Harlequin and Silhouette, our category contracts are fairly standard and don't have a lot of room for negotiation, which means an agent can be less of a necessity than in other types of publishing. However, agents will get a writer beyond the query letter stage, and good agents—ones who know the genre and publishing and believe in their authors' work—can be an asset to an author's career.

□ **What do you want submitted from a first-time author?**
We need to see a complete novel from a first-time author before we go to contract so we can be sure that the author has the ability to sustain a story and to finish a novel. We will give writers feedback prior to that if we're interested in a proposal.

□ **Why are you so willing to work with new authors?**
We have a very strong package. Readers will try books by authors they have never read before because it's a *Silhouette Desire* or because it's a *Special Edition,* because that package and that brand offer them a guarantee of a particular type of story. They'll take a risk with a new author, a risk that very few people would be willing to take on a single title and very few publishers ever take in general publishing.

□ **Is category romance a good opportunity for writers?**
We publish over 360 books a year in Silhouette alone. If you like the genre and you like the books, it's an incredible opportunity for writers.

□ **What kind of money do writers of romance fiction earn?**
Advances for an unpublished author probably range between $2,000 and $5,000. However, the advance is against royalties, so each author ultimately earns what she sells.

Some of our authors, who write consistently and well, have been able to make a living at their writing, which I think is pretty impressive. However, it can take years to build a solid career, and our advice is, "If you sell your first book, please don't quit your day job."

□ **What do you think of authors who want to write romantic fiction just for the money?**
Authors who go into it for the money are a waste of our time. They are competing with authors who are totally committed to writing the best books they can, who love the genre, love their readers, and really want to do well. Compared to that commitment, somebody who says, "I think I can make a lot of money tossing this off on the weekend" just doesn't measure up.

□ **Do your authors receive media attention?**
Yes. We have a local author publicity program, and a lot of authors do their own publicity. They get newspaper, television, radio—everything. Several Silhouette and Harlequin books have even been turned into TV movies.

□ **Tell me about your book contracts.**
They are pretty standard. It depends on the author. We may do a multibook contract with an established author who has a strong performance record. For other authors, we go book by book.

□ **What about royalties?**
We offer escalating royalties that begin at 6 percent, based on the cover price of the book.

□ **Do you have pet peeves?**
One of my pet peeves is writers who think that they can intellectually manufacture emotion and storytelling ability. Lack of professionalism and commitment are others.

□ **Why is category romance writing special? Why would you recommend it to an author?**
Once we buy an author, we want to develop an ongoing relationship. We want to see her next book and the book after that. Three-fourths of our authors have sold us second books. Many authors write three to four books a year, and many have sold more than ten books to Silhouette. Three writers have recently published over fifty books with us, and the number is growing. I work with one author who has written more than sixty books with us in ten years.

When an editor develops a relationship with an author at Silhouette, both are committed to achieving a shared vision—making the reader happy and selling books. It's a very unique editorial and publishing experience.

□ **Do you have advice for writers in search of a publisher of category romance fiction?**
Write what you love. Be passionate and be professional. The key ingredient, however, is storytelling ability. You have to make a reader want to read your story. A particular challenge for romance writers, in addition to creating charismatic characters and an effective plot, is the writing. You're packing a lot in a small space, and you have to be able to tell the story in a very compelling and readable manner, which is very difficult. As one writer said, "Just because category romances are easy to read doesn't mean they're easy to write." In fact, it's quite the reverse.

A winning romance captures the readers' emotions. The capacity to make readers laugh and cry is a must for romance authors. The ability to strike an emotional chord is something that an editor can't help an author do. I can help an author make sense and create consistent characters and a coherent plot, but I can't make that magic happen. That has to come from the author.

42

Women's Romantic Fiction

JEANNE TIEDGE, SENIOR EDITOR
Warner Books, Inc.
New York

JEANNE TIEDGE, Senior Editor at Warner Books, double-majored in English and French in college. After graduation, she worked at a New York literary agency, then moved to editorial in 1984 at New American Library, where she rose from assistant editor to senior editor. In 1987 she became executive editor at Popular Library, a division of Warner Books. When Popular Library folded a year or so later, Tiedge was promoted to senior editor at Warner. Her specialty is women's romantic fiction. Tiedge has worked with renowned romance writers such as Sandra Brown, Barbara Delinsky, and Susan Kyle, who is known in the category romance world as Diana Palmer.

Warner Books, a division of Time-Warner, Inc., publishes hardcover, mass market, and trade paperback books. Warner publishes about twelve women's romantic fiction titles a year, one each month. According to Tiedge, Warner is relatively small in size and monthly output. "We probably pack a bigger punch for our size in the number of best-sellers and authors," she says. "What we lack in volume, we make up for in the total sales."

Women's romantic fiction is mainstream, commercial fiction. Tiedge is not interested in and doesn't publish any category fiction romances.

☐ **How does romantic fiction differ from category romantic fiction? (See also chapter 41)**
Nothing in mainstream, commercial romantic fiction is written to formula. We don't have any tip sheets or guidelines. We don't have various book lines that we

publish on a monthly basis. Category romances are shorter than mainstream and do not have the scope of story and characterization.

□ Is romantic fiction a large segment of publishing?

Romantic fiction overall—I believe this includes category as well as mainstream romantic fiction—makes up about 46 percent of the total mass market paperback sales. This is the largest segment, profit-wise, of the mass market publishing industry. General fiction comes next.

□ What are your criteria for a winning commercial mainstream romance novel?

I don't have any. It is a very subjective decision on my part. A successful commercial mainstream novel must be multilayered. The plot cannot just focus on the romance itself. I want very strong minor characters in subplots who have their own story to tell, which may or may not reflect back on the main characters. The depth and the scope of the story have to be truly broad and mainstream in terms of detail. Other than that, I know it when I see it.

□ What kind of story are you looking for in a romance novel?

I'm looking for stories about ordinary people who find themselves in an extraordinary situation and become extraordinary as a result of their involvement. You could pick out most of the women and a lot of the men in the stories that we publish and say, "I know that person," or, "I could imagine myself in that position."

□ How do you acquire most of your books?

Through agents who know what I like. Once in a while, and more frequently with nonfiction, through recommendations from my authors.

□ How can an unagented writer get to an editor?

Call and ask for the name of an editor who specializes in your area of interest and send a query letter to that person. That happens quite frequently. I've had my name listed in the acknowledgments of books. A good, succinct query letter should be no longer than a page, should include a statement up front about what the book is, what area of fiction or nonfiction it falls into, the writer's credentials for writing this particular book, especially for nonfiction, and one paragraph summarizing the plot. If the author has a one- or two-page synopsis, he or she should attach it. But that's it. If I like the query, I'll ask for three chapters and a full synopsis. If we like that, we'll usually ask for the whole manuscript.

□ Will you ask for the entire manuscript before a contract is offered?

Absolutely. Even for people coming out of category who want to write mainstream fiction. While I know they can write a 55,000- or 60,000-word category romance, I want to be convinced that they can write a full-bodied, multidimensional novel. The two are very different.

□ What credentials are you looking for in an author?

Many of the people who do contemporary mainstream romantic women's fiction have come from a category background. They've written at least ten to twenty category romance novels, have somewhat of a following, and have hit some of the chain best-seller lists. They have some momentum behind them and they're now ready to be broken out into the next level. When we take on a first-time author, there has to be something extraspecial about him or her that we can highlight in terms of publicity.

□ Where should first-time romance writers break in?

Writers trying to break into romance benefit from being part of an established program. They get something that we can't give them initially when published at a company that has a specific line, because publicity is built in and around that line. A new writer truly benefits from such inclusion.

□ What kind of money do authors of mainstream romance novels make?

It varies. I wouldn't say any advance is lower than $5,000, but from there it can go up to tens of thousands and hundreds of thousands of dollars. It depends on the author's success. Royalties start at 6 percent, based on the cover price of the book.

□ Is romantic fiction popular because sex sells?

That's been totally disproven. An area of controversy over the last several years has centered around cover art. Conventional publishing wisdom has dictated that the clinch should go on the cover of all romances because sex sells and that's what women are really reading these books for. Readers and writers have disputed this for years and are asking that stereotypical, derogatory images be taken off the jackets. That has started to happen within the last couple of years. It is a trend that I don't see going away and that I think is very beneficial for the genre. A lot of the jackets are still feminine looking, but they're not overtly sexual, giving the impression that all that's between the covers is eroticism.

□ What is the educational level of your readers?

The category publishers have done this type of research. I believe that the last study suggests that over 50 percent of the readers have at least some postsecondary education. The majority of them own their own home. The majority of them work at least part-time.

□ **How does** *The Bridges of Madison County* **fit in the romantic fiction area?**

The Bridges of Madison County has to stand aside from everything I've said because it was such an atypical book for Warner to publish at the time. But that book came in, editors read it, and said, "We don't do first novels, this breaks all the rules, but we love this book." The novel comes up when I go to romance conventions all the time. "If this book had been written by a woman, would it have been taken seriously?" they ask me. That book, to me, is not your traditional romance. For one thing, it doesn't have a happy ending. Even the romantic women's fiction that we publish still have happy endings in terms of the main romance working out. *The Bridges of Madison County* doesn't. It's adultery, which is not a conflict typically associated with romance. The book is written from the male point of view. Rather than a romance, *The Bridges of Madison County* is a story of the love that got away—something that anybody, whether you're twenty or eighteen or sixty, might experience. Essentially, it's about forfeiting love, as opposed to striving to make it work.

□ **Why aren't there romance books for men?**

I don't know. Men's romance is probably different. One could argue that *The Bridges of Madison County* is a romance book from a man's point of view. Or that men's romantic fantasies tend to be romance with a capital R, in the guise of Louis L'Amour western romance.

□ **Do you have advice for authors of romance novels?**

I like to see very professional attitudes. For instance, if you sent me three chapters and a synopsis and I asked to see the rest of the manuscript, I expect to receive that manuscript.

If you're sending out multiple submissions, let me know in the cover letter.

Get manuscripts in on a timely fashion. If you know you're going to be late, give me plenty of notice.

It's important to research any publishing house thoroughly in terms of what types of books they publish. Read books that have been currently published by a particular house to get a sense of where your book might or might not fit in. Different publishers do have different profiles in the business. If you've researched the company and you can cite some of our authors and compare or contrast your book—"I'm writing to you because you're the editor for Sandra Brown, and I think that I'm writing very much in her vein"—then you're going to catch my attention.

If a book is turned down, you should just let it go. It's not a good idea to start a letter campaign to everyone else at the company. I recently turned something down and cited editorial and marketing problems as part of the reason. The author wrote to various department heads in other parts of the company, trying to get them to reconsider. That was extremely unprofessional. At that point, the rest of the people at Warner never wanted anything to do with the potential author. That was a gross faux pau.

Treat publishing as you would any other business. Just because you're working out of your home and you have more flexible hours than other people, you still need to project a very professional image.

43

Books for Children and Young Adults

STEPHANIE LURIE, VICE PRESIDENT, EXECUTIVE DIRECTOR

Simon & Schuster Books for Young Readers
New York

STEPHANIE LURIE is vice president and executive editor of books for young readers at Simon & Schuster. After graduating from college with a major in creative writing, Lurie started her publishing career as sales coordinator at the now defunct company, Dodd, Mead. From there she moved to Little, Brown and Company's publicity department. She switched to editorial early on and she climbed the ladder from editorial assistant to senior editor over a period of eight years. She moved to Simon & Schuster in November 1993.

Simon & Schuster is the country's largest publisher, the children's book division publishes 160 books a year in both fiction and nonfiction.

☐ **Please describe the major children's book categories.**
Traditional picture books for children ages four to eight contain anywhere from zero to two thousand words. They are thirty-two or forty pages long in printed book form. They are usually read to the child.

Early readers or easy readers are slightly longer picture books. Instead of thirty pages in a printed book form, they are forty-eight or sixty-four pages. There are a few simple sentences on each page. These are for children who can now read by themselves.

First chapter books are designed for seven- to nine-year-olds who have progressed beyond early readers but are not yet ready for full-length novels. These books average sixty-four to eighty pages in printed form, about thirty typed pages or six thousand words in manuscript form.

Middle-grade novels are written for eight- to twelve-year-olds. The manuscripts run about 15,000 to 25,000 words. Sometimes we put a few black and white interior illustrations in these books.

The young adult age group is twelve years and up. Young adult books usually don't have illustrations. They come in at about two hundred manuscript pages.

□ **Should authors submit artwork with picture book proposals?**
We say, "If you are a writer, stick to writing. Don't worry about the illustrations." The publisher likes to hire the artist.

□ **What if the author is an illustrator with strong writing skills?**
That's great. We encourage author/artists. They can send in a dummy with sketches, text in place, and a sample piece of artwork.

□ **Who creates baby books that are predominantly illustrations?**
Ideally, a baby book should originate with an author/artist—someone professionally trained in art, who has a good idea and can write a very simple text. We're not going to pay much money for a text that may consist of one word per page.

□ **What if two people, a writer and an artist, collaborate on a proposal for a picture book?**
That's fine. People must understand that we may say, "We love this writing, but the art isn't polished enough." Or, vice-versa, "We love this artist, but the writing is weak."

□ **What range of advances do you offer writers and illustrators of children's and young adult books?**
It depends on their individual experience and name recognition. Advances vary according to the individual's experience and how commercial we feel the project is.

□ **How do you usually acquire books?**
I acquire the majority of my books from authors who have been published before. We are also committed to developing new talent, however.

More doors are open to new writers in children's book publishing than in adult publishing. Authors of adult books need an agent just to be read. About 50 percent of our authors are agented.

□ **How do you decide whether a book fits into your publishing program?**

It's individual taste—what the editor gets excited about. We look for things that are either highly commercial or extraordinarily literary, work that would earn starred reviews and awards.

□ **What do you look for in an author?**

Professionalism. Creativity. A willingness to take constructive criticism and apply it to his or her work. The ability to revise. Realistic expectations about marketing.

□ **What does an ideal children's book proposal include?**

A short cover letter with information about the author's background and why the idea is marketable.

For nonfiction, authors should include their intention for the book, an outline, three sample chapters, and a comparative book list that analyzes the competition.

For a novel, a cover letter and a synopsis with three sample chapters is great, but we're also happy to look at the entire thing. We're interested in the author's take on the subject—why she chose the idea, why it spoke to her, why she thinks there's a market for it. The letter will tell us a lot about an author's writing ability, too. We try to read manuscripts all the way through and give each one a fair chance.

We're looking for the writer's credentials, a subject that hasn't been covered but would have wide interest, a brief description of similar works, and how this book would fit into the market.

□ **Why do writers need credentials?**

They are most important for nonfiction. For instance, if someone wants to write about substance abuse in children, he should have firsthand knowledge of the subject and/or a related degree. Credentials make the book more salable. When the library market was our major outlet, writers could choose any subject they liked, research it like a book report, and publish it. Now the library market is smaller and we have to sell to many other outlets. Books have to be more specialized than ever before. Relevant credentials give a book an extra edge.

□ **What story lines do you want in young adult books?**

We want an idea that is fresh and hasn't been done a million times before. Or it can be a tried-and-true idea approached from a new angle. Today, the market for young adult fiction is very limited. We're looking for writers who are trying innovative styles and different points of view—the same kind of sophistication that people are looking for on the adult side.

□ What types of fiction do well?
Multilayered stories with many characters—adult characters as well as children—and each one is fully developed. Complex plots with symbolism. The novels take a very distinctive character with a problem we've never seen before. We like to see the way it's unraveled or solved.

□ What makes a book stand out?
It's hard to define what works. The writing must be superb, the idea fresh, and the story multilayered. We're always looking for that extra spark of humor or imagination. The biggest problem today is that we can no longer afford to publish the "good old-fashioned read"—boys' adventures or something like that. We're looking for material that will rise above the competition.

□ What constitutes a successful young adult book?
Books that sell 7,500 to 12,500 copies in the first year. Or the book that wins a Newbery award and sells 100,000 copies.

□ Do children's books receive major media attention?
Not unless it wins a Caldecott or Newbery Award, or it is written by a celebrity, or it is on a special, trendy nonfiction topic. We rarely do national tours.

□ What is the major market for your books?
Our books are sold in bookstores and libraries. The market for hardcover fiction is almost strictly libraries. There's a limited amount you can do to change that.

□ Does anyone publish paperback fiction for young adults?
Yes, several mass market and trade houses publish paperback originals, but we don't as yet.

□ Do you participate in auctions for books?
Yes. It rarely happens with novels, because they just don't sell in a way to warrant an auction. But a big, splashy gift book or a name author with good sales expectations may be auctioned by an agent or foreign publishers.

□ Do you have pet peeves?
I've seen people submit manuscripts full of errors, or dog-eared copies that look like they've been around forever.

Some people have unrealistic expectations about the time it takes to consider a book. We try keep it down to three months. Some authors say, "Can you get it back to me in two weeks?" That's unreasonable, considering how much we have to do.

Sometimes writers say, "I'm willing to go on 'The Today Show' to promote my novel." That doesn't happen with children's books.

□ **Do you have advice to authors in search of a children's book publisher?**

The first thing to do is make sure the idea really sings to you—that it's coming from the heart and is not written to satisfy a certain trend or to sell to a certain market.

Once you have a good idea, research the competition and appropriate publishers. Then take time to write and polish your piece.

Get feedback from other writers and revise accordingly. Market your piece using the knowledge you gained during your research.

A lot of authors are nervous about simultaneous submissions, but most publishers accept them, realizing that ours is a competitive business and we can't expect authors to wait forever. I recommend submitting a proposal to as many publishers as it would be appropriate for.

Epilogue

Many editors enter publishing with a dream. Some fantasize stumbling on a blockbuster, as Maureen Egen did with her discovery of *The Bridges of Madison County*. Others imagine working with the next Hemingway or F. Scott Fitzgerald. Those dreams are often shattered by the reality of a fast-paced, bottom line publishing business.

As I interviewed editors, I glimpsed a world I never imagined—a world of deadlines, bottom lines, and all-out stress. I learned that editors would like nothing better than to deal personally with every writer. But, usually, they can't. They're just too busy. An editor's workload can be awesome. As Rick Horgan bemoaned, "It can be suffocating. It can exhaust every hour of your day." When editors don't respond in a week or two to a query or a book proposal, it's not that they don't want to or don't care. They just don't have time. Their tremendous workload often takes away from what they would prefer to do: read books and work with writers.

I hope that readers of this book will come away with a better understanding of editors, editing, and the publishing process. If knowledge is power, we writers should now have the power to get published.

ABOUT THE AUTHOR

Judy Mandell is the author of numerous feature articles, with subjects ranging from kicking caffeine to how to get published, for major magazines and newspapers. Her books include *Magazine Writer's Nonfiction Guidelines* (McFarland & Co.), *Fiction Writers Guidelines* (McFarland & Co.), *Golden Opportunities: Deals & Discounts for Senior Citizens* (Thomassan-Grant), *The One Hour College Applicant* (Mustang Publishing—coauthored), and three computer handbooks. She has lectured about getting published and taught "Creative Approaches to Publishing" at the University of Virginia.

Mrs. Mandell is a graduate of Cornell University. She has two sons, one daughter, two daughters-in-law, and one grandson. She lives with her husband, Jerry, lots of tropical fish, and two huge dogs in North Garden, Virginia (near Charlottesville).